How to Slackline!

How to Slackline!

A Comprehensive Guide to Rigging and Walking Techniques for Tricklines, Longlines, and Highlines

Hayley Ashburn

Photos by Scott Rogers

FALCONGUIDES

GUILFORD, CONNECTICUT
HELENA, MONTANA
AN IMPRINT OF GLOBE PEQUOT PRESS

FALCONGUIDES®

FalconGuides is an imprint of Globe Pequot Press.

Falcon, FalconGuides, and Outfit Your Mind are registered trademarks and How to Climb is a trademark of Morris Book Publishing, LLC.

Interior photos by Scott Rogers unless noted otherwise.
Illustrations by Robert Prince unless otherwise credited.

Project editor: David Legere
Text design and layout: Casey Shain

Library of Congress Cataloging-in-Publication Data

Ashburn, Hayley.
  How to slackline! : a comprehensive guide to rigging and walking techniques for tricklines, longlines, and highlines / Hayley Ashburn ; photos by Scott Rogers.
      pages cm
  Includes index.
  ISBN 978-0-7627-8499-8
  1. Mountaineering. 2. Rappelling. I. Title.
  GV200.A835 2013
  796.522—dc23

                                                                                    2013013569

Printed in the United States of America

10 9 8 7 6 5 4 3 2 1

Contents

Chapter Three: Longlining 93

Chapter Four: Highline Skills 131

Chapter Five: Highline Rigging 159

Glossary 183

Knots Index 186

Index 191

About the Author 197

About the Photographer 198

Introduction

Slacklining was once relegated to the select few climbers who had the knowledge and gear to rig a slackline from scratch. Today slackliners come from all backgrounds. The introduction of easy-to-assemble slacklines has transformed slacklining from an obscure offshoot to a full-fledged, modern extreme sport. However, while the mass production of slackline kits has produced a new generation of highly skilled balance athletes, it has also left those athletes ill-equipped to think critically about slackline rigging and to manage the full array of rock climbing gear needed to safely construct a longline or highline.

I was lucky enough to be part of a community of rock climbers and slackliners that were, at the time, pushing the limits of slacklining, but it still took me years to learn the ins and outs of slackline rigging. Today I know just about every trick there is to rigging and walking slacklines, but the majority of that information is still passed from slacker to slacker by word of mouth and remains difficult, if not impossible, to learn without the help of an experienced slackliner.

Owing to the infinite variety of slackline styles and locations, no book could ever cover every specific slackline rig. Each slackline is unique, the materials and methods determined by the nature of the anchors and style of the rigger. The purpose of this book is to explain the applications of the most common slacklining gear, and to put in simple terms the time-tested techniques for rigging safe, walkable slacklines in a variety of environments.

There is no "right" way to rig a slackline. American highline guru Terry Acomb describes the phenomenon like this: "If you ask four different slackliners how to rig something, you'll get five different opinions." Slackline rigging is not a standardized practice. The type of line you rig will be determined by the type of line you like to walk. That's what makes slacklining so wonderfully personal, and so difficult to learn. Each line is customized by the slackliner who rigged it. Talking with other slackliners about rigging preferences is one of the best ways to learn more about slackline rigging. Studying this book will give you the tools to weigh in on slackline rigging discussions and form opinions of your own.

How to Use This Guide

Slackline rigging and walking are progressions that go hand in hand. This guide moves through slackline concepts in ascending order of complexity and difficulty, assuming that the reader has no prior knowledge of slackline gear or rigging techniques, and working up to more advanced rigging and

Jordan Tybon walking a highline in the Fisher Towers, Utah

Once slacklining was for experts only. Today children are one of the biggest sectors of the slackline community. Kids as young as 2 and 3 can enjoy bouncing on the line with their parents.

walking by building on concepts explained in earlier chapters.

Start by learning how to walk a lowline, then get familiar with slackline gear and start rigging your own lines. More advanced slackline walking techniques are paired with chapters about rigging advanced lines. You don't even need to think about how to walk a highline until you can confidently rig a good longline.

This guide includes all the technical information you need to make informed decisions about what gear to invest in, including detailed descriptions of what gear is out there, what will work for slacklining, and how to use some of the newest innovations in slackline gear. What follows is a set of guidelines that provides a framework for safe slackline rigging illustrated by real-world examples and photos.

You will learn how to build a custom line that reflects your personal walking style while adapting to the specifics of any given location. You will learn how to build safe slacklines and to judge what is safe enough by evaluating the consequences of failure. You will learn how to make your rigging safer as you master longlining and highlining, in that order.

If you are looking for information on a specific topic, including knots, flip to the glossary and knots index in the back of the guide.

Ethics

Slackliners have a special relationship with trees. No matter how good you get at slacklining, you will always be able to find a pair of trees that challenge your abilities. The problem with trees is twofold: (1) They are alive, and (2) somebody owns them. City officials across the United States are debating the slacklining issue because of the potential for damaging trees in public parks. One of the major goals of this guide is to set a standard for rigging that makes it easier for public officials to condone slacklining.

Slackliners need to understand that our lines put a great deal of force on trees, and can damage or even kill trees that are too small. Even big trees need to be padded before affixing anchors. You don't have to be a hippy to care about the trees, pad your anchors, and police your friends; if you don't, slacklining could be banned in your hometown.

The second best slackline anchor, after trees, is a set of bolts. It's easier to place a bolt than it is to think creatively about how to use natural anchors. Unfortunately, bolts are permanent, and slackliners may unwittingly put bolts in a taboo location (such as in the middle of a climbing route or within sight of a hiking trail). Use this guide to learn alternate methods of rigging. It is considered extremely poor style to place a bolt where you could have rigged to a boulder or tree instead.

Talk to someone at the crag to learn local customs, and research the rules and regulations of

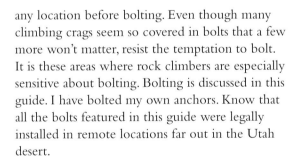

Richard Webb walking a line using proper tree protection on the anchor

Here, I'm paying my dues on Andy Lewis's world-record tower highline: Leviathan

any location before bolting. Even though many climbing crags seem so covered in bolts that a few more won't matter, resist the temptation to bolt. It is these areas where rock climbers are especially sensitive about bolting. Bolting is discussed in this guide. I have bolted my own anchors. Know that all the bolts featured in this guide were legally installed in remote locations far out in the Utah desert.

Critical Thinking and Community

What this guide cannot provide is a checklist for how to rig a safe slackline. For that you will need to think critically about gear and analyze locations as you find them. The best way to learn that skill is to find a good slackline mentor to follow around and learn from. I was lucky enough to have slackline legends like Andy Lewis and Mike Payton as my mentors, along with a whole tribe of experienced slackliners and climbers from around the world. Some of what I learned from them is in this guide; a few even weighed in with opinions about how to rig and walk their favorite lines. I am forever indebted to them for teaching me not only how to walk but also how to rig slacklines. They saved me from my own sketchy rigging on numerous occasions; it's always good to have someone else around to double-check your work.

You will need to find your own slackline tribe—people who love to slackline and argue about gear. Don't be afraid to approach experts; they always need more backs for carrying gear, and it won't matter to them if you can't rig or walk the line. Just bring a big, empty backpack and I promise you'll be welcomed with open arms.

Scott Rogers walking the Lost Arrow Spire Highline, one of the world's most historic lines

The History of Slacklining

You may think of slacklining as a new sport or as something that is just now catching on. While balancing on webbing is a relatively new invention, rope walking has been around in some form or other since at least the Roman times, and likely earlier.

Tightrope

Reportedly, tightrope walkers put on spontaneous performances high above the streets of Rome and even in the Coliseum. The Romans called these artists *funambula,* and today funambulist is the technical term for wire walkers, tightrope walkers, and slackliners.

Ancient plaster paintings, buried for 1,700 years under the same volcanic ash that buried the ancient city of Pompeii, depict what look like small demons walking on what are unmistakably tightropes stretched over A-frames, a structure slackliners still use today. This discovery stretches the written (or painted) record of tightrope walking as far back as AD 79.

Tightrope walking is not only an old sport, but also a global one. Historians can't say how long the Korean tradition of Jultagi has been around, but it may have begun as early as 57 BC. Now considered part of Korea's cultural heritage, Jultagi is a unique form of tightrope walking where performers combine acrobatic performance with music and acting.

A group of Gibbon athletes visited Korea in 2010 to appear on a television show about the similarities between slacklining and Jultagi, and were shocked to see traditional Jultagi performers doing many tricks very similar to those in slacklining. A between-the-legs butt-bounce is now named "The Korean" out of respect for a culture that has been performing it for more than 2,000 years.

Across the globe, at the wedding of Charles VI to Isabel of Bavaria in 1385, a funambulist reportedly walked high above the royal wedding feast.

A modern-day Jultagi performance in Jeonju, South Korea
WIKIPEDIA COMMONS

Rope walking was popular all over Europe for centuries, but didn't make it across the Atlantic until the first American circus in 1793.

Decades later, in 1859, Charles Blondin of France elevated rope walking to a high art when he made the first daring crossing of Niagara Falls on a single 3-inch hemp cord. Blondin walked the 270-foot-high and over 1,000-foot-long line blindfolded, on stilts, even pushing a wheelbarrow—all with no safety harness or net of any kind.

Highwire

Until 1800 the term "tightrope" was correct, because artists used ropes. Tightrope walking is the art of walking on a rope tensioned between two points. However, what people usually mean nowadays when they say "tightrope walking" is highwire walking.

The Flying Wallendas were the first act to make human pyramids on the highwire, with as many as nine artists on the wire at a time.
KARL WALLENDA

Tightrope walking was much more difficult and dangerous than highwire walking. Around 1800 the Industrial Revolution advanced to a point where reliable cable was readily available, and most circus performers switched to rigging with this steel wire instead of the traditional round rope or cloth cord. This was the beginning of highwire walking, and artists could now perform much more technically difficult and eye-popping tricks like building human pyramids and riding bicycles across the wires.

The modern highwire is made of a steel cable that is between ⅝ inch and 1 inch in diameter.

Highwires are tensioned and stabilized with supportive wires called guy wires, or cavalletti wires. Wire walkers commonly use a weighted pole for balance. The pole Philippe Petit used to walk the highwire between New York's Twin Towers was 26 feet long and weighed fifty-five pounds.

The most iconic highwire walker in history is probably Karl Wallenda of the Flying Wallendas, a famous circus act that began in Milan in 1922 and continues to perform today. By the age of 16, Karl Wallenda, their founder, was doing handstands on the shoulders of a German wire walker 40 feet in the air. Karl would go on to make tightrope walking world famous as an act in the Ringling Brothers Circus. At a performance of the Flying Wallendas in Acron, Ohio, in 1935, a guy wire came loose, causing Helen Wallenda to lose her balance and fall from the top of the pyramid. She was miraculously saved by Karl, who stunned the crowd by catching her between his legs as he hung from the high wire by both hands.

After that, wire walking was largely ignored by the press until Philippe Petit illegally rigged and walked a wire between the Twin Towers in 1974. After nearly ten months of planning, Petit and a few trusted accomplices snuck into the Towers disguised as construction workers and shot the wire from one tower to the other using a bow and arrow. Petit walked the line at dawn on the morning of August 7 and, in his words, "linked [the towers] for eternity."

Slackline

On the opposite side of the country, in Yosemite Valley, California, the story of balance was taking a different path, toward what we now know as slacklining. Modern slacklining evolved here from the rich climbing culture. To challenge themselves and improve their balance, rock climbers experimented by walking on chains, slackwires, climbing rope, and, eventually, webbing.

Pat Ament and others had been walking slackwires and ropes since as early as the 1960s in a Yosemite Valley campground called Camp 4, and the story of their coming home from long days at the crag to balance on chains around this campground has attained the status of legend in the slacklining community. The camp is still there; sadly, the chains and slackwires are not.

Slackwires and slackchains seemed to be unique to Yosemite Valley, but even there the activity remained nameless until Jeff Ellington and Adam Grosowsky found a way to rig tubular webbing and add tension with what is now called the "primitive system" or the "Ellington system." A precursor to

today's pulley and ratcheting systems, the Ellington utilizes search and rescue techniques, replacing pulleys with climbing carabiners to create a mechanical advantage.

In 1985 Scott Balcom broke Philippe Petit's record for highest line (formerly the Twin Towers at 1,368 feet), rigging and walking the famous Lost Arrow Spire Highline. Perched between a granite cliff and delicate finger of stone some 2,890 feet above Yosemite Valley, this highline has become the most famous and sought after in the world.

Now slackline athletes are pushing the limits every day. In 2008 professional climber, slackliner, and BASE jumper Dean Potter jumped from a highline wearing a parachute. Dean performed the stunt over a canyon in Moab, Utah, calling it the world's first BASEline (in which you make a BASE jump off a highline).

Another important figure in the history of slacklining is Andy Lewis. Following in Potter's footsteps, Lewis free soloed the Lost Arrow Spire Highline and BASE jumped from a highline in Moab, not far from the location of Dean's original BASEline. Andy's career took off when he landed the first ever slackline backflip in 2006. Footage of his Squirrel Backflip went viral, appearing in a Nike commercial and inspiring trickliners around the world. Lewis invented most of the tricks performed at competition level today including the double drop-knee, the modern butt-bounce, and the chest-bounce. He also hosted one of the first ever tricklining competitions in Humboldt County, California, in 2008. The Humboldt Classic is still held in California every year.

Around this time competitive slacklining started to shape and expand the slackline community, similar to rock climbing or skateboarding. In 2007 Robert and Jan Kaeding developed the first simplified slackline kit in Germany and started the first slacklining company—Gibbon Slacklines. Gibbon focused on building the slacklining community with events and slackline competitions. The

The first ever World Cup Series in Brixen, Italy, 2010

ANDY LEWIS COLLECTION

high-tension slackline kits were really the beginning of high-level trickling. For the first time, athletes from many nations were meeting each other at competitions like the Slackline World Cup in Germany. The Internet also played a large part in the rapid growth of slacklining. Slackliners all over the world used forums, social networking, and YouTube to share knowledge about tricks as well as rigging. Youth and adults in Japan, South America, Europe, the United States, and Canada started contributing their tricks both in person and online, allowing the World Cup to become a truly global event.

As trickling evolved and competition trickling started introducing increasingly challenging and technical tricks drawn from skating and parkour, the sport moved beyond its sideshow status and became something Americans wanted to get better at. Since 2008 the number of people slacklining in the United States has more than tripled.

The first Gibbon World Cup was held in 2011 in the United States, and other competitions are held by groups like the San Diego Slackers and Slackline Visions in Colorado. Slackline clubs are forming on college campuses like Ann Arbor, Berkeley, and the University of Colorado. There are now slackliners in almost every nation in the world, and people are drawn to the sport because it's cheap, accessible, and exciting.

Tightrope walking is not just for circus performers anymore.

The Evolution of Gear

It all started with rope walking. Men and women were once brave enough to trust their lives to handmade hemp rope suspended high above the ground. Rope walking is the true mother of slacklining. Like slackliners, rope walkers used ropes simply anchored at each end, with no guy wires and no pole for stabilization. This was the only way to perform aerial acts until 1800, when steel cable was invented.

Steel cable brought the advent of what most people think of today as "tightrope walking," a word that is generally misused. The performers you think of as tightrope artists are actually not walking on rope at all, but a wire. The wire is a steel cable anchored not only at each end, but also from guy wires attached at intervals along the wire. These smaller wires stabilize the line and prevent most side-to-side movement. Guy wires effectively separate a highwire into several shorter sections. So while a 100-foot slackline is much more difficult to walk than a 15-foot slackline, a 100-foot highwire avoids this problem by dividing the line into shorter lengths.

Synthetic nylon was invented in 1935, but it took a long time for climbers to discover its utility as a balance line. The 1960s and 1970s saw a huge increase in the popularity of climbing in the United States as well as advances in the technology available to climbers. One particular mountaineering method, known as the Tyrolean traverse, is probably the origin of the first slackline rigging. If a team of mountaineers needs to cross a large gap between two cliffs, they set up and anchor a wire to both cliffs, then clip their harnesses to the wire and slide across, safely suspended over the abyss. The methods of tightening, anchoring, and harnessing are nearly identical to what you would see if you watched a modern highline outing. The difference is that with slacklining you are walking over the line, rather than hanging beneath.

Rope walking has a long and rich history, and while it certainly inspired the idea of slacklining, the backyard slackline wouldn't exist without the climbing world's advanced gear and a few fearless mountaineers leading the way. New equipment such as nylon webbing and pulleys are drawing huge crowds to slacklining; the sport is technically easier than rope walking, and there is no need for heavy spools of steel or the complex construction required of highwires. Today is an exciting time in the history of funambulism, because the equipment has finally evolved to a point where everyone can try it.

The Styles of Slacklining

Slacklining, by definition, is the act of balancing on a piece of webbing that is tensioned between two points. However, as slacklining technology advances and athletes take the sport in different directions, the traditional definition becomes inadequate. Slacklines are rigged and walked at radically different heights, lengths, and tensions. Some of the lines are so different from one another that people consider them a separate sport.

Following are a few different types of slacklining; keep in mind that these are just outlines. Part of what makes slacklining special is that athletes can customize their own slacklines, developing a unique style and rigging a line to complement it.

Making it look easy as I perform a Buddha pose

Tricklining

Tricklining is as example of lowlining. Trickliners use low, short lines to practice tricks. These tricks aren't necessarily impossible on higher or longer lines, it's just a lot scarier and more dangerous at a greater height. The standard trickline is low and tight, and incorporates elastic webbing, which gives power to jumps and softens landings.

Modern slacklines make it possible to perform flips, butt-bounces, and 360s on the line. The increasing popularity of this type of slacking attracts skaters, parkour runners, and gymnasts, who all bring their own style into the mix, transforming tricklining into a competitive sport.

Tricks are divided into two types:

Static: Tricks like the drop-knee, the splits, or simply sitting on the line are considered static. These are slow-moving or still-pose tricks where the slacker stays on the line.

Dynamic: Jumping, rotating, and butt-bouncing are dynamic tricks where the slackliner catches air, leaving the line and landing again without losing balance. Some slackliners can even land flips.

This guide will discuss how to rig a trickline in detail. The important factor for tricklines is that they are very tight. Your best choices for gear are a Gibbon slackline kit or a set of pulleys. See the next chapter for more on selecting the right gear.

Toru Osugi performing a dynamic trick during a Gibbon Slacklines competition

Andy Lewis in Tippy-toes Buddha—a static pose on a Gibbon slackline

Yoga Slacklining

Set apart from tricklining by its slow, calming style, yoga slacklining focuses on breathing and concentration. Yoga poses such as Warrior and Tree can be performed on slacklines, as well as handstands and cartwheels. Everyone knows a little yoga—try a lunge!

Practicing yoga on the slackline can add a new level of difficulty to your yoga routine. For slackliners without a yoga background, this slackline style will help you tap into your focus. Nothing quiets the mind better than a few minutes spent in deep concentration on the slackline.

There is no special "yoga slackline." Build whatever line you like, and try some yoga on it. A yoga slackline is generally a little looser than a trickline, and it's more common to practice on 1-inch webbing rather than 2-inch.

Cassie Frantz performing the Dancer pose on a slackline

Urbanlining

It's not always feasible to go to the park to slackline. Slacklining in the city using urban anchors like bridges and telephone poles, and public structures like fountains and playgrounds is called urbanlining. It's a fun way to get out into the city and do something uncommon. Slacklining on city property is not illegal, but usually frowned upon, so urbanliners have to rig, walk, and take down their line before the authorities even notice they're there. A team of slackliners famously rigged, walked, and de-rigged a slackline across a city street in the time it took for the traffic light to change from green to red and back again.

The best lines for urbanlining are Gibbon slackline kits, because you can put them up and take them down again quicker than any other type of line.

Steffi Seidel busting a move on an urban anchor
PATRICK RIFFEL

Longlining

Once you've mastered the trickline-size slacklines, you will probably want to see if you can walk something longer. The longlining branch of the sport focuses on building lines that are long—often longer

than 100 feet—and working to break personal records. The first official longline world record was set by extreme climber and photographer Heinz Zak. He set the record in 2005 at 328 feet (100 meters). Today, due to advances in webbing technology, the record has ballooned to 1,621 feet, held by Jerry Miszewski, who walked it on Vectran webbing. Faith Dickey holds the women's world record of 728 feet, walked on a polyester/Dyneema webbing.

Rigging longlines requires a lot more time, investment, and knowledge than your average backyard slackline. You will need pulleys, heavy-duty steel carabiners, and a substantial amount of webbing. See the chapter on Longlining for more on how to get started.

Highlining

Highlines refer to slacklines that are higher than they are long, or any line where a fall is likely to result in injury or death. Highliners build lines high on mountains or above canyons and walk across with a climbing harness and a safety rope called a leash. A safety ring slides along the line behind the walker, linking the leash to the highline. When a highliner falls, the only consequence is a big, long swing that leaves him or her hanging several feet below the line.

The basics of highline rigging and walking are included in the final chapters of this guide. This arm of slacklining is *for experts only.* It will take more than a guide to learn the ins and outs of complex anchor building for highlines. You must put in time rigging longlines, tricklines, and lowlines of all sorts before you can begin rigging highlines. After reading this guide, if you still want to get involved with highlining, the best thing you can do is apprentice with an expert.

Andy Lewis attempting a 494-meter longline, the current world record
HAYLEY ASHBURN

Scott Turpin walking a highline on Longs Peak, the highest elevation highline on the continent

CHAPTER ONE

Finding Your Balance

I n my experiences teaching slackline, I often hear people refer to their "sense of balance," as in "I have a terrible sense of balance." Thinking of balance as a sense is limiting because it is very difficult to improve our senses; however, humans have a huge untapped potential to improve their physical balance. Balance must be practiced, honed, and maintained to tap into this potential, but through diligent training it is certainly possible. The skill of balancing requires a combination of senses working together to let us know where our bodies are located in space. There are three distinct sensory inputs that function together to help us balance: vestibular, tactile, and visual.

The vestibular system is composed of a number of liquid-filled canals in the inner ear. Liquid moves in these canals like water in a level, stimulating small hairs to transmit information regarding the angle of our bodies in relation to gravity. Spinning in circles causes the liquid in the inner ear to change position as a result of centripetal force; this is why we feel dizzy after spinning around in a chair or on a roller coaster.

How do you compensate for dizziness? Usually by putting out a hand to stabilize your body like a tripod. When one component of the balance system is compromised, the human brain compensates by adding sensory input from another component, in

this case the tactile component. Simply standing is a basic function that requires tactile data. Under normal circumstances the sensation of both feet on the ground provides more than enough information for our brains to maintain our bodies' balance while standing. When we feel dizzy, putting out a hand can help us regain our balance because it adds more data for the balance system to compute.

Slacklining is difficult because the amount of sensory data our brain receives from our feet is reduced on a slackline. Only a small surface of webbing (about 1 inch wide) comes into contact with our feet when we slackline, as opposed to a surface completely covering the soles of both feet when walking on the ground. Learning to balance on a slackline basically involves developing the skill to balance using less sensory data. This explains in part why it is so much easier to balance on a slackline when holding onto a partner's hand. The hand provides extra tactile data to compensate for what's lost to the feet.

The third and often least understood component of the balance system is visual. It seems obvious that we determine where we are located based on information from our eyes. If you woke up somewhere unfamiliar, you would immediately look around to get your bearings. However, the relation of visual input to the balance system is less

Finding balance in the looming darkness

intuitive. New slackliners constantly look down at the ground when trying to balance, but this is wrong. It is the horizon line that tells our brain which way is up and how to balance. You must see where the ground is in relation to the horizon and the trees and the slackline, in order to effectively balance in space.

Try balancing on one leg. Where do your eyes rest? The eyes are invariably drawn to a space on the ground several feet in front of the body. Try balancing looking directly down at your feet, then try balancing with eyes completely closed. Both are much more difficult than letting the eyes rest naturally in a place where they can take in data regarding the horizon, ground, and surrounding objects all at once. Waterlines and highlines wreak havoc on the visual component of the balance system; practicing on these lines will enhance your natural capacity for balance by training your mind to function with limited data.

Balance Training

As mentioned, balance is not a sense, it is a skill— one of the most undertrained skills in athletics. Improving your capacity for balance has a whole host of benefits. Originally slacklining was used to train balance for rock climbing, but balance training on a slackline can improve performance in any sport that requires basic coordination.

Golfers: Want to improve your swing? Any golfer will tell you that the key to a consistent swing is to maintain your balance and swing with a smooth rhythm. How can you hit hard while looking graceful like a pro? Balance is the key, and slacklining can help you understand how to coordinate the rest of your body, balance-wise, while executing a powerful swing.

"The successful warrior is the average man, with laser-like focus."
— Bruce Lee

Skiers and Snowboarders: These sports are all about maintaining a stable center of gravity while reacting instantly to changes in speed and terrain. The key is maintaining a center point of balance from which any maneuver is possible. The US Ski Team as well as many professional snowboarders are using slacklines to train the muscle memory and enhanced reaction time they need to stay balanced on the slopes.

Skaters and Surfers: It's notoriously difficult to simply stay on top of the board in these sports. Slacklining can help maintain a fluid sense of balance while executing difficult maneuvers. Think a kick-flip is hard? Try a butt-bounce, and train your mind to perform faster and more accurately in situations where balance is precarious.

Martial Artists: The martial arts are one of the oldest sources of balance training. How can you overcome an opponent? By knocking him off balance. Balance training has an immediate and obvious application in the martial arts: stay balanced or be defeated.

These are just a few examples of activities where slacklining can directly improve performance. Balance is one of the most neglected areas of athletic training, and honing your balance skills with slacklining can take you to the next level in any sport. The strength you gain in your core and the focus you learn in your balance practice will improve your performance in everything from next week's softball game to your upcoming physics exam. The range of applications for slackline training is endless: core strength, focus, balance. These are the qualities of any elite athlete, and are exactly what is gained from training on a slackline.

Walk the Line

This chapter lays out a pretty large set of rules for just standing up. Keep in mind that these are pieces of a larger picture. If you described any physical motion one part at a time, it would sound complicated.

Most of these guidelines apply even when you're walking to the fridge for some leftovers, but you'll notice you don't need to flag your arms out then. All you are doing by slacklining is adding a degree of difficulty that forces you to keep the natural posture your body is designed to stay in all the time.

Quinn Carrasco walking a line in Golden, Colorado

Preparing

You've chosen your line, selected your anchors, and rigged, but are you ready to walk? Remember, slack-lining is a mental game as much as a physical one. Once your line is rigged, don't forget to take a few deep breaths and really focus on the task at hand.

Your line: Should be rigged somewhere as quiet and private as possible, low to the ground (try knee level) and no more than 25 feet long.

Your body: Should be stretched and relaxed. Try warming up. Stretch your hamstrings, calves, and back. Do some slow, deep breathing with your eyes closed to still your mind.

Your shoes: Should be removed if the ground is soft enough. You don't want to step on sharp rocks when falling, but the more of the line you can feel, the better. If you must wear shoes, they should be closed-toe sneakers with relatively flat, thin soles.

Your head: All the above is really about clearing your head. If you feel prepared and at rest, focusing on the line will be much easier.

Mounting the Line

Slacklining is a slow-moving sport. The slower you move, the better. When you think of mounting the line, don't worry about the idea of walking. Just focus on standing up on the line as an entirely separate movement.

Stand close to the line and center your body directly over the webbing.

Slowly shift your weight onto the line and raise your arms.

1. Start very close to the line, as this will set up your center of balance over the line.
2. Place your dominant foot on the line, toes facing forward. This is the foot you would naturally use to kick a soccer ball.
3. Slowly shift your weight from the foot on the ground to the foot on the line. Don't worry if the line seems a little high; it will sink a lot as you put your weight on it.
4. Raise your arms above your head and stand up. Keep your arms relaxed and above your head, with your elbows at a 90-degree angle. Your arms should be neither fully extended above your head nor completely to the side.

Walking

Walking is not really a single action, but rather a slow shift between two standing poses, from standing on the left leg to standing on the right.

1. To avoid looking down, feel for the line with your toes before putting your weight on it.
2. You won't have trouble keeping your toes pointed forward if you don't rush. Slowly shift from standing on one foot to the other.
3. Try to relax your upper body. Being too tense will stop your breathing and make it harder to swing your arms.
4. Hang your hands limply from the wrist. Your forearms and hands should be relaxed and ready to swing left and right.
5. If you feel like you're going to fall, bend your knees and refocus on your breathing.

Walking with my arms relaxed—notice the limp wrists and bent knees

Common Issues

WHY IS THE LINE SO SHAKY?

You will have to focus on controlling the shake as you learn to walk, but as your legs get stronger, eventually the shaking will subside. You'll develop muscle memory, and controlling the line will become reflexive. In the meantime:

1. Try leaning forward (not hunching) as you step onto your front foot. Your weight should help control the shake.
2. Bend your knees.
3. Don't be afraid. Slacklining requires confidence.

Terry Acomb on his backyard slackline. Try a smile if you're having trouble relaxing.

HOW CAN I MAINTAIN FOCUS ON THE LINE?

If you are struggling to clear your mind, there are a few techniques derived from meditation that might work. Every slackliner has a different method. Here are some common ones:

- Try a mantra. Recite a power word such as "breathe" or "control" on each step.
- Count each step.
- Listen to music while walking.
- Breathe loudly through your mouth (my personal favorite).
- Go somewhere quiet and uncrowded to practice.
- Calm your mind with yoga stretches before getting on the line.
- Visualize yourself walking the line.

HOW DO I MOUNT THE LINE IF IT FEELS TOO HIGH?

For higher lines, try standing up while holding someone's hand. More advanced slackliners can try a Chongo mount:

1. Face the far anchor and place your back foot on the webbing, perpendicular to the angle of the slackline. Bring this foot very close to your body and shift your weight onto it; put your front hand on the line for stabilization.
2. Keeping your weight back, bring your front foot onto the line and let go of the webbing, using both arms for balance.
3. Shift your weight forward and stand slowly.

A Chongo mount:

Step 1   *Step 2*   *Step 3*

The Four Unbreakable Rules of Slack

In my experience people stay on a slackline for any number of reasons, but they fall off the line only if they break one of these four rules:

1. Eyes forward
2. Toes forward
3. Hands up
4. Breathe

Toru Osugi demonstrates how not to follow the four rules of slack.

Eyes Forward

Slacklining is all about learning how to balance with less access to sensory data. When you're walking on the sidewalk, it makes little difference where your eyes are focused, but on a slackline it is crucial to train your eyes forward, perhaps on the anchor. Your feet have only a few points of contact on a slackline, rather than an unlimited surface from which to collect data, as on the sidewalk. Focusing on your vision helps the balance system compensate for your newly "blind" feet.

Whatever you do, don't look down!

Try closing your eyes and balancing on one foot to appreciate how important vision is to the balance system.

When walking a slackline, the anchor need not be your only option for focus. You could look at the tree, the line ahead, or any other stable point. Whatever you choose to concentrate on, try to remain aware of the slackline and the horizon. Maintaining some peripheral awareness of these objects is crucial to orienting your body.

The only thing you should *not* look at is your own feet or the line directly below you. Looking down moves your head from a balanced position resting on your neck, to an unbalanced hanging position. Think of looking down like trying to walk the line holding a twenty-pound bowling ball around your neck. Lastly, keeping eyes forward, on the anchor or other nearby object, helps you stay focused on your goal. If you're looking at your dog or a cute guy or girl walking by, you will lose your focus and fall!

Toes Forward

You can think of this rule as "staying square." Foot position is simply the foundation for a squared body. Foot position determines hip position, which affects shoulder position. All three are important for keeping your body symmetrical, or "squared," above the slackline. Start by keeping your toes pointed forward or slightly out, and keeping your hips and shoulders squared to the end of the line.

Try imagining an invisible wall rising from the length of the slackline. Your center of balance (behind your belly button), your head, and your foot on the line should all be aligned within this plane. Your shoulders and hips should be perpendicular to the wall, half of each on either side of the plane. If any part of your body crosses through the plane, you've lost symmetry and are about to fall. Keeping your toes pointed out keeps your body aligned symmetrically in the plane.

With toes crossed, this slacker is headed for a fall.

Your feet should look like this on the line.

You can see that this slackliner has approximately even parts of her body on each side of the line.

Hands Up

A scale balances when it has equal weight on each side of the fulcrum, or the center.

You can use this same principle to stay balanced on a slackline. Keeping your hands up helps maintain equal weight on either side of the line.

When walking, your body will naturally move the line left or right; swinging your arms compensates for this motion, equalizing the weight on either side of your center of gravity. By keeping your hands relaxed at head level, your shoulders are always in a symmetrical position, and your arms are ready to move immediately.

Cassie Frantz walking with a squared body position, hips and shoulders aligned in a square facing forward toward the anchor

Breathe

Archery, martial arts, running, golf, yoga, and many more sports emphasize the importance of breath and its impact on performance. Without oxygen the muscle cells in the body cannot work.

Nevertheless, many beginners hold their breath. Breath is an involuntary function of the body, but it is also intimately connected with the mind. Anxiety and fear cause tension and elevated heart and breathing rates. These changes negatively impact motor coordination, focus, and center of gravity.

Deep breathing reduces blood pressure and heart rate, reducing anxiety and bringing more energy to the cells of the body. It also relaxes your upper body, allowing the arms to flow and react like they need to.

Your breath will provide a point of focus for the overactive or fearful mind. If you feel like you're falling, breathe louder and more intentionally. Deep breathing will focus, relax, and energize you all at once. Breath is absolutely the key to slacklining and balance.

You can always tell when a slackliner is struggling because he makes a face as if he's ready to blow out a cake full of candles. Here, Ray Marceau focuses on his breath to maintain balance on a highline.

Slackline Is Not a Crime

Though slackline is growing rapidly, slackliners are still the minority when it comes to using public parks and other recreational areas. This means that slacklining in public can become a spectacle because it is still unusual enough to attract a crowd in most places. This level of attention can be fun, slacklining is a great conversation starter, and you're likely to meet many new friends. However, it also means that slackliners are subject to more scrutiny than other park visitors. Many cities have rapidly growing slackline communities, which raises concerns that too much slacklining will damage city trees or create a safety hazard in the park. City park officials in particular have a difficult time deciding what to do about slackliners. Some cities across the United States have preemptively placed bans on slacklining. Once a ban is in place, it can be extremely time-consuming and difficult to have it removed.

It is much easier to avoid a ban in the first place by slacklining responsibly. You may already

Andy Lewis staying off the grass

Andy Lewis flipping for a couple of police officers in Humboldt, California

JENNA MCLENNAN

have noticed that slacklining in cities and parks can quickly make you the center of attention. As members of a small community, each slackliner effectively acts as an ambassador for the sport. Your actions when you are in the spotlight directly affect the public's perception of slackliners in general. If you make yourself a nuisance, you might find yourself stuck with a slackline ban in your city. If you follow a few basic guidelines for slacklining ethically, you'll create a positive perception of slackliners that helps the sport grow and prevents city officials from turning slacklining into a crime.

City officials and other community members are usually concerned about the same three issues wherever slacklining is becoming popular: damage to city property (or the environment in general), disrespect to other park visitors, and the creation of a safety hazard.

Protect the Trees

The tree you're anchoring to could be older than you are. Show some respect! Always protect trees with padding under the anchor slings and judiciously select trees that are large and healthy for

I wonder if this tree is thick enough . . .

Protect the Environment

- Slackline on durable surfaces—dry grass or packed dirt is best. Avoid wet grass (it can become a mud pit), woody-stemmed plants, landscaping elements, or anything else that might be damaged by heavy traffic.

- Don't leave trash behind, including cigarette butts and pieces of slackline tape.

your slackline. Trees are often the biggest concern for park services because they are valuable and difficult to replace.

If you're slacklining in an urban environment, try not to damage any public property. Test your urban anchors well before slacking; bending parking meters or breaking railings is a sure way to convince the cops that slackliners are a menace.

Be Courteous to Other Visitors

Remember that you're not the only person trying to enjoy the park. Be considerate about where you rig your line. Using trees on opposite sides of the park for a longline might seem like a good idea, but on a sunny afternoon you'll disrupt every other sport in the area. A single slackline can cut through a space that would normally accommodate several small games of soccer and frisbee, so save the longline for a weekday morning or an overcast day when the park is less crowded. If you can't wait, take your slackline somewhere more rural to practice.

Consider bikers and skateboarders when choosing a slackline location. Never rig a slackline over a bike path or sidewalk, and remember that bikers can cut through grassy areas too. Bikers are moving fast and may not see your slackline in time to stop!

Be Safety Conscious

Besides keeping yourself safe on a line, slacklining in a crowded area forces you to think about keeping others safe too. Consider the location of your slackline carefully. Slacklines can be difficult to see from the side; cyclists and pedestrians have a bad habit of clotheslining themselves on slacklines, especially when the webbing is at eye level. Keep your slackline away from any pedestrian crossings or bike paths.

Never leave your line unattended. You are responsible for everything that happens on your slackline during the time it is rigged. Leaving a slackline unattended increases the chance of someone running into it. You don't need to hold everyone's hand, but you should watch new slackliners on the line to make sure they can handle themselves, especially when novices are attempting longlines. Some lines just aren't safe for beginners; it's good to be friendly, but you are not obligated to let every random stranger attempt your longline. Sometimes it's your responsibility to simply guard the line, especially when kids are around. Other people's kids should be treated with extreme care. Parents have a habit of wandering off when their kids get really engaged by the line; try not to let this happen. Children should only slackline on your gear one at a time and with parental supervision.

One day slacklines may become as commonplace as Frisbees in the park, and most people will ignore them. Until then slackliners should expect to attract extra attention. Every slackliner, like it or not, is an ambassador for the sport when they slack in a crowded area. Most people who approach you have never seen a slackline before, and many will ask questions and expect you to talk about the sport. Before you get annoyed, remember that we all started out as spectators. Most of us would never have learned how to balance if a friendly stranger hadn't answered our questions and invited us to stand on his or her line.

Timmy O'Neill walking a slackline stretched completely across Chautauqua Park
HAYLEY ASHBURN

Community

Slacklining is a social sport—half the fun is simply having a reason to get together with friends. If you've got your own slackline, don't be surprised if other slackliners approach the line and take steps without asking, even if you've never met. You've just made a new friend. It's an unspoken rule of slacklining that a rigged line is an invitation; remember that the next time you walk by a stranger's line. Slacklining is an open sport, and it's important for your own progression to meet other slackliners. Try to find people who challenge your abilities and introduce you to new slackline opportunities.

Don't be shy about meeting other slackers, asking for help, or sending a message to your favorite slackers online—you can always count on a friendly response! In turn remember the community ethic when someone else wants to walk your slackline or ask you about rigging. There's no better sport for meeting people, slacker or non-slacker.

Community is the most important ethic in slacklining. Getting involved in the slackline community means not only making more friends, but also improving your skills. Maybe it comes from the rarity of the sport, but one slackliner is usually always glad to meet another, and that's how the community grows. Sometimes meeting just one person who's already involved is all it takes to find your local slackline community. Doors will open and you'll quickly find yourself with six new friends at your first longline or highline, just because you were brave enough to approach your fellow slacker.

Working together to practice some longlining techniques

Three Good Ways to Find Other Slackliners in Your Area

USE THE INTERNET AS A RESOURCE

The slackline community is very Web-based—the Internet will be your friend here. Slackline.com was one of the first resources specifically designed to promote community; you'll find other slackers here as well as events and information about gear, rigging, and community news. Facebook is good for finding slackers you already know, or looking up a well-known athlete and watching their videos.

Watching slackline videos is one of the best ways to improve at tricklining. YouTube has a constantly updating selection of slackline videos, and if you're not involved in your local community just yet, this is the place to see the newest slackline tricks performed by the pros, as well as by slackers from around the world.

GO OUTSIDE AND SLACKLINE

Invite your friends, coworkers, family, classmates, neighbors, and so forth. There are a lot of people out there curious about learning how to slack, and if nothing else it's an amazing excuse to hang out in the park on a nice day. Build your own slackline community. Slacking in the park is a great way to meet people; everybody's curious, and odds are, a fellow slacker will jump on your line at some point.

LOOK FOR LOCAL EVENTS

Check your local climbing gym, yoga studio, or university for slackline events and groups; these places often have a permanent slackline set up. With the sport growing in popularity, climbing gyms like The Spot in Boulder, Colorado, have begun hosting slackline-only nights and devoting entire areas to slacklining. Now there's even a slackline-specific gym called Bridges in the Bay Area, offering slackline instruction to the rapidly growing community around San Francisco.

Slackline Rigging

Anatomy of a Slackline

A slackline is a very simple system defined as a piece of webbing tensioned between static and dynamic anchor points. All slacklines—from beginner ratchet kits to highlines—are composed of five main elements: primary anchor points, anchor slings, webbing, line lockers, and a tensioning system. Changing the particulars of each element can create an enormous range of lines, but the fundamental design of a slackline always remains the same.

Primary Anchor Points: Primary anchor points are the foundation upon which a slackline is built. Trees are the most common primary anchor points for slacklines, but rocks, bolts, and man-made structures can also serve as slackline anchors. Select anchor points in different locations to rig a waterline, urbanline, or park line. Set anchors high to walk a highline, or far apart for a longline.

Anchor Slings: Use anchor slings to wrap a primary anchor point and link it to the slackline system. Anchor slings are integrated into the webbing and ratchet on commercial slackline kits. For more complex slackline setups, a range of materials and methods can be used to wrap primary anchor points.

Webbing: Different varieties, lengths, or widths of webbing will change the way a slackline feels.

Line Lockers: Made from simple hitches, ring and carabiner combos, or slackline-specific hardware, line lockers link both ends of the webbing to the anchors without using knots.

Tensioning System: Pulleys, chain hoists, and ratchets are the most common tensioning systems for slacklines. Ratchets are the simplest tensioning system to rig, but also the least powerful. Use pulleys or chain hoists for rigging longlines, 1-inch lines, and highlines.

Static and Dynamic Ends: Slacklines are basically a symmetrical system, with two each of the above components, except the tensioning system, on either side. The main difference between the two ends of a slackline is that one end holds a tensioning system between the anchor and the line locker. The side with the tensioning system is called the dynamic end, because the position of the line locker on this side will change. The side without a tensioning system is the static end.

Rigging a slackline in Thailand

Putting together the pieces of the puzzle

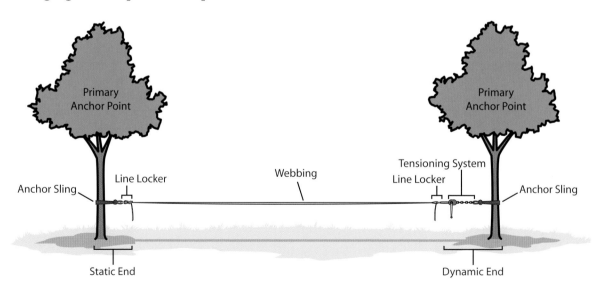

A slackline broken down into its major elements

Choosing Your Gear

When I bought my first line, I pieced together climbing and rescue gear to build each element of the slackline and pulley system. Luckily for the modern slackliner, custom slacklining kits and slackline-specific gear make it easier than ever to get started slacklining. Now you can walk into most outdoor stores and buy a prefabricated slackline kit right off the shelf, or, if you are looking for a more versatile slackline, you may choose to build your own system. Even if you are familiar with climbing gear, buying your own slackline setup can be

The Monkey Den gear pile

Choosing gear to bring up to the line

confusing. Both "primitive" setups with carabiners and slackline kits with pulley systems require an assortment of materials. This chapter will cover several different setups to give you some idea of the available options. Choosing which is the right line for you should be pretty simple after we go over a few gear basics.

Primitive Line with an Ellington Tensioning System

This is the slackline design used by the original Yosemite Valley monkeys in the 1970s. The system is called "primitive" because the technology is, well . . . primitive. Made entirely from climbing gear, this slackline setup uses only basic non-locking climbing carabiners and the friction of the webbing to create tension.

GEAR

- Four non-locking, oval climbing carabiners (you must use carabiners designed for climbing)
- 70 or more feet of 1-inch webbing
- Anchor material
- One rappel ring
- Tree protection

WHERE TO GET THE GEAR

Buy the pieces separately wherever outdoor gear is sold, or choose a kit at online slackline stores like slacklinebrothers.com or balancecommunity.com.

WHO IS IT FOR?

"Primitive" lines are ideal for anyone who wants the challenge of a looser line, or climbers who already have some of this gear lying around. Primitive lines work for tricklining, yoga slacklining, and any kind of freestyle slacklining.

UPSIDE

This line is soft and squishy, which is a feel many slackliners prefer. It costs marginally less than slackline-specific gear, and it's the most lightweight system around. It's also extremely durable.

An Ellington kit

DOWNSIDE

Your line will always be a little loose. The mechanical advantage of the Ellington pulley system is far less than that of real pulleys or a ratchet. This means that you'll never get these lines tight enough for dynamic tricks like big jumps, and you'll need to work much harder to pull the slack out of your line.

Ratcheting Slackline Kits

While "primitive" slacklines and 1-inch kits are typically designed for low-tension, ratcheting slacklines are made to be very tight. The most common ratcheting slackline kit is the Gibbon slackline, which consists of a ratchet and 2-inch nylon webbing. A ratchet is a hand-crank device that makes it relatively easy for one person to tension the line. Kits usually come with two looped ends, eliminating the need for separate anchors and carabiners.

GEAR

- Slackline kit
- Tree protection

WHERE TO GET THE GEAR

Look for kits at REI, Amazon.com, Gibbon-slacklines .com, or anywhere climbing equipment is sold.

WHO IS IT FOR?

Ratcheting kits are perfect for anyone over the age of 5. The design is super simple for this reason—it's meant to bring slacklining to non-climbers. This type of line is great for fitness-oriented slackliners, beginning walkers, and parkour-style trickliners. It is also a good choice if you will be slacklining alone a lot. Basically, ratcheted lines are perfect for almost everyone. The 2-inch webbing and relatively powerful tensioning system create a stable, wide slackline that's ideal for learning to walk and beginning to execute jumps or tricks. Ratcheting slackline kits can be placed extremely low to the ground, making it safer for kids and easier for adults to learn how to walk. The line can be set up in a matter of minutes, making it a good choice for beginning riggers.

UPSIDE

"I've literally seen a monkey do it."

This is the easiest and simplest slackline to set up. There are only two pieces. The ratchet generates very high tension, which is a key feature for practicing dynamic tricks, making Gibbon slacklines, in particular, the most popular slackline for tricklining. In fact Gibbon slacklines are probably responsible

1-Inch vs. 2-Inch

All Gibbon slackline kits come with 2-inch webbing, and most pulley kits or primitive kits come with 1-inch webbing. Like the tension you choose for your line, choosing between 1-inch and 2-inch webbing depends on your level of experience and personal style.

Two-inch webbing has a wider surface area, and some people believe this makes landing jumps or simply walking a lot easier. This kind of line can tip side to side, but overall has very little movement or "sway."

One-inch lines can be set up longer than 2-inch lines. They also have more sway and require more balance to stay on. Highliners, longliners, and yoga slackliners almost always use 1-inch lines.

Which is better? Slackers have been debating that since the 2-inch line became popular, and everyone has their own opinion. In the end it's really like choosing between a mountain bike and a road bike: It all depends on how you want to ride it.

for modern tricklining, because the system makes it easier to land jumps or tricks.

The ratcheting kits are not much heavier than a primitive system, which means that your slackline can go wherever you go.

DOWNSIDE

Ratcheting kits can only be extended to about 100 feet max, so they are not usable as longlines. They're a little heavier than a primitive system, and sometimes ratchets jam if used improperly.

Slackline-Specific Pulley Kits

Slackline pulleys used to be for advanced riggers only, but today slackline-specific pulley kits have made rigging with pulleys possible for slackliners of any experience level. Pulleys are the most versatile option for tensioning any type of slackline, from short, low-tension beginner lines to high-tension lines as long as 200 feet for aspiring longliners. Pulley systems are attached to one end of the slackline, between the line locker and the anchor, and pulled with a rope to tension the webbing. A "brake" locks the rope in place, preventing the slackline from de-tensioning once you let go.

A Gibbon trickline kit
FRANKIE NAJERA

GEAR

- Slackline-specific pulley kit

WHERE TO GET THE GEAR

The only slackline-specific kit sold today can be found at slacklinebrothers.com. For information on building your own pulley system using climbing gear, see the discussion on pulleys in the Longlining chapter.

WHO IS IT FOR?

Slackline-specific pulleys are a great buy for slackliners who want to eventually advance to longer and higher lines. They are also ideal for settings where a slackline will be set up for a long time in one spot and the focus is on durability of the system. While it's not necessary to put pulleys on a line shorter than 30 feet (a ratchet or primitive system will work just fine), if you want a very high-tension 1-inch line, longline, or highline, slackline-specific pulleys are your best option.

UPSIDE

Slackline-specific pulleys are the most diverse of any preassembled slackline kit. Pulley systems can be used on the widest range of slacklines, from tricklines to highlines. This means your kit can grow with you as you advance through the levels of slacklining. They generate enough tension for lines as long as 200 feet but are most useful in the 50- to 150-foot range, and can be used on either 1- or 2-inch webbing. This equipment is powerful and durable. Pieces can be easily ordered and replaced, and one pulley kit should last several years or more.

DOWNSIDE

What slackline-specific kits gain in durability, they often lose in efficiency. All pulleys exhibit some form of friction on the rope as a slackline is tensioned. Slackline-specific pulleys such as the Slackline Brothers pulleys have a mechanical advantage of 4:1, but some of that advantage is lost in friction between the rope and the pulleys. Very advanced slackliners and longliners will want bigger pulleys for longlining. Bigger pulleys have reduced friction and therefore are more efficient. Additionally, the steel Slackline Brothers pulleys are heavy, and this kit is bulkier than a ratchet or Ellington kit.

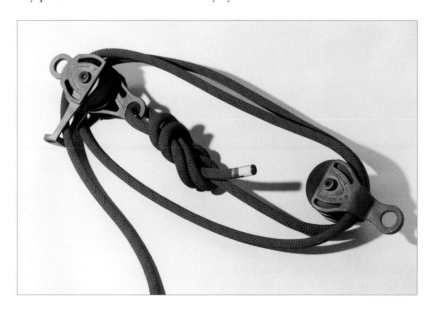

A Slackline Brothers kit

Selecting Slackline Anchors

Regardless of what kit you're using, you will need two strong trees or other anchors for your line. These are called primary anchor points, and they must be extremely strong. Slacklines have been known to break masonry, pull volleyball nets over, and deform metal. Use caution when selecting anchor points, and never trust any primary anchor point outright. Carefully inspect all anchors, and be aware of any sounds or movement that occur during tensioning and slacklining.

TREES

The vast majority of slacklines are rigged to trees. They make great slackline anchors and can be found almost anywhere. The problem with trees is that they are living things; this means slackliners must be extremely cautious in their rigging practices.

Not all trees make good slackline anchors, and many are too weak to hold a slackline without bending or breaking. You don't have to rip a tree out of the ground to kill it; simply putting too

So you think that tree looks strong enough? Imagine it holding a Smart Car suspended from the anchor sling instead of a slackline. Do you still feel good about it?

much force on a tree can cause it to eventually wither and die. Trees come in many shapes, sizes, and conditions. Use your judgment when selecting trees for slackline anchors, and always err on the side of caution.

When evaluating a tree, look at the following factors:

- Make sure the tree is big enough to inspire confidence. Generally a tree should be at least as wide as your thigh.
- Give the tree a shake test. If you can make the upper branches and leaves move by shaking the trunk, the tree is not solid.
- Look at the roots of the tree and make sure it is sitting in an adequate amount of soil. A tree is only as strong as its roots, so if it is living in extremely rocky or shallow soil, or if it's boxed in by lots of pavement, find another anchor for your slackline.
- Make sure the tree is alive and well established. Both dead and newly planted trees have a tendency to rip out of the ground at the roots.
- Consider the bark. Trees with thick, flaky bark are more susceptible to damage than those with thin, smooth bark; try to avoid them.
- Know whose property the tree is on before you anchor to it. The property owner will probably know more about the condition of the tree than you can infer from looking at it.
- Know the local rules and regulations; some cities do not allow slacklines to be anchored to trees in public parks.
- Pad your trees well with thick carpet scraps or towels, or custom treewear from a slackline manufacturer. Protection between the anchor and the sling is crucial when rigging to trees. A slackline rigged without padding can seriously damage and even kill a tree.

I can't stress how important it is to use caution when anchoring slacklines to trees. Damaged trees can get slacklining banned from your city parks for good! Anchoring to inadequate trees or forgetting to pad your anchors makes it harder for slackliners everywhere to convince city officials to permit slacklining in public parks. There are plenty of trees that are more than strong enough to hold a padded slackline anchor without sustaining any damage. If you're unsure about the condition of a tree, don't use it as an anchor. Be vigilant during tensioning; if you hear any creaking or see movement around the roots during testing or tensioning, switch trees immediately.

URBAN ANCHORS

Anything man-made can be classified as an urban anchor. Slacklines, and even highlines, have been successfully rigged on everything from handrails to skyscrapers. Once you start rigging your own lines, you'll begin to see slackline anchors everywhere. It can be really fun to rig slacklines on unusual urban anchors, and sometimes urban anchors are the only available option.

STRUCTURALLY SOUND

In construction, objects are considered structurally sound if they can withstand any forces that are *likely* to be put on them. Slackline forces are never anticipated. A slackline puts force on anchors at a 90-degree angle, while most urban structures are designed to withstand force from above. Builders are not expecting sideways forces when they evaluate the structural soundness of any given object.

Consider the intended purpose of structures when evaluating them for slackline anchors. If the structure is designed to support cars, large buildings, or any type of heavy-duty lifting, it should be strong enough to support many times the weight of a slackline, regardless of direction of pull. However, objects like street signs, parking meters, and handrails are usually designed to support no more than their own weight, and are much more likely to bend or break when pulled in odd directions.

Light posts are not designed for load-bearing applications. This one seems well anchored, but rigging the line any higher would be testing fate on this questionable urban anchor.

PATRICK RIFFEL

The difficulty with evaluating urban anchors stems from the inconsistency of construction methods. Many urban anchors *are* built to be more than structurally sound. A handrail may surprise you with its strength. When evaluating urban anchors, notice the materials used and the foundation of the structure. A solid steel handrail that is well anchored in a large concrete block will probably work well as an anchor. A handrail that sounds hollow and is merely bolted to the pavement is probably not solid. Always avoid brick structures and anything with drywall or molding. Regardless of how strong the interior, drywall and molding will crush under tension.

The anchors that work best tend to be structural supports for massive buildings and roads. Look for giant, exposed metal beams anchored in concrete, and concrete pillars. Anything that holds up a bridge or skyscraper is probably good; railings intended to block automobiles from driving off the road are generally solid too. Construction cranes and tractors can be trusted, but not cars and trucks. The truck may stay still, but whatever part you wrapped your anchor around is likely to detach from the body of the vehicle. Don't trust anything outright. You will need to think critically and test your anchors before you use man-made structures for slackline rigging.

Testing Urban Anchors

Every urban slackline anchor should undergo three tests: visual, physical, and practical. Start by inspecting the anchor visually—how big is it? Does it look cracked or broken? What material is it made out of, and how well is it anchored? Next, try a physical test. Use your body to apply as much force as possible to the object. Can you make it move by pushing or pulling on it? You shouldn't be able to sway, shift, or tip anything you plan on rigging from. The last test is practical. See what happens when you actually rig your slackline and tension it. You're not going to ever generate much more force on your slackline than during tensioning, so if something goes wrong, it will probably happen then. Listen carefully and watch your anchors for movement. Have a friend stand at the opposite anchor so that both sides can be observed. If your anchor creaks, proceed with caution. If you hear any cracking or popping sounds, or if you feel your anchor move, abandon the mission. Usually if an anchor can withstand the tensioning test, it will be solid, but if it does anything that makes you feel uneasy, it's probably best to find another anchor point. A big fall or aerial trick can sometimes break anchors that seemed solid during tensioning.

Anchors to Avoid

- Signs
- Most handrails
- Anything with molding or drywall on the exterior
- Volleyball nets
- Tennis nets
- Parking meters
- Flagpoles
- Most diving boards
- Basketball hoops
- Fences
- Masonry of any sort

Rigging Fundamentals

Physically putting all the pieces of your gear together to build a slackline is called rigging. Rigging is a creative process: Every slackline is different, and you'll want to build different kinds of slacklines for different groups or locations. However, no matter what kind of line or where you're building it, there are only four basic variables to consider: protection, height, angle, and tension—or PHAT. If you remember PHAT, you can build a fun, safe slackline every time.

Protection

Protection refers to the padding around your anchor point that protects your line from damage and potential failure.

It's important to remember protection first, because it goes *under* your line; once you rig and tension the line, it's too late to add protection. Whether you're rigging from trees or urban objects, the webbing of your slackline will eventually begin to wear down near the ends from friction on the anchor; sometimes a sharp edge can even snap your line! Using protection keeps your line looking and performing like new.

Demonstrating some basic slackline rigging techniques

Height

You will need to choose a height at which to set your line. This depends on three important factors:

1. Who is slacklining?
The skill level of your group will determine the height of your line. Lower lines are better for beginners, who will be falling off the line a lot. Setting your line too high is a sure way to scare off beginners. On the other hand, if you set your line too low, it might bottom out or touch the ground when weighted in the middle.

Don't forget protection!

2. Where?

Consider the surface under your line. Hard surfaces like concrete and packed dirt are going to *hurt* if you fall off the line from more than 3 or 4 feet. Rig your line accordingly.

3. How long is the line?

Length dictates the height of your anchors to some degree. Consider the shape of a slackline with a walker balanced in the middle: It's a very shallow V. The center of the V will hit the ground if you place your anchors too low; this is called bottoming out.

The longer the line, the higher you'll need to set your anchors. If you want to rig lowlines, you must keep them short. You can set a ratcheting slackline kit as low as 1 foot off the ground, but only if it is no longer than around 10 feet long. Waist height is ideal for most lines under 50 feet long. If you want to walk a longer line, you'll need to rig the anchors higher.

Angle

There are two angles to consider when rigging a slackline. The first is the angle of the slackline between the trees. Good slacklines are level. You can achieve this by having a partner look at your line from a distance, or by measuring the height of the first anchor placement and rigging the second to match. I do this with my body. If I stand next to the first anchor and it's at belly button height, I'll rig my second anchor to belly button height too. Watch out for sloping ground when you do this; if one anchor is uphill, the measuring technique won't work.

The second angle to consider is the angle of the webbing itself. Because webbing is a flat material, it matters how you orient your line in space. Webbing that tips to the side as it approaches the anchor can be disconcerting for slackers, and webbing that makes a full twist is even worse.

When you stretch your webbing between the anchors, run it through your hands and ensure that the webbing lies flat for the whole length of the line, with no twists.

Preventing tilt is more difficult. The tilt of the line is determined by the orientation of the webbing where it connects to the anchor. On ratcheting slackline kits the loop and fold method is used to control the angle of the webbing as it passes through the anchor loop. For all other slacklines a line locker holds the webbing flat, and the tilt of the line locker is determined by a carabiner connecting the anchor to the line locker. If the carabiner is tilted, the line will tilt. You'll learn how to prevent this in the simple anchors section.

Tension

A slackline without tension is like a moped without gas. You can still pedal it around, but it won't go far or very fast. Stretching webbing tight between two anchors gives it completely different, and awesome, properties. Tensioned webbing is easier to walk; it opens up possibilities for jumping and bouncing tricks; and it makes spanning large distances possible.

Slacklines can be walked at any tension. A slackline with no tension is called a rodeo line, and a slackline with lots of tension is a trickline; discovering all the types of lines in between will be part of your slacklining adventure. Usually slackliners settle on a preferred tension, but I encourage you to experiment with the tension of your line. There is no correct tension for any given slackline—it just comes down to personal preference.

Before the line is tensioned, anchor slings, padding, and hardware have a tendency to shift and fall to the ground. After tensioning, it can be difficult if not impossible to readjust these items. Any knots tied in the system will cinch tight, making them tough to untie after holding slackline tension.

Think ahead and prepare for tensioning your line. Double-check all your gear to ensure that it is correctly placed before pulling tension on the slackline, and consider having a partner hold in place

The Crotch Rule

This is a rigging concept that sounds funny but can make or break your slackline experience. Try to build your slackline no higher than the shortest person's groin. This ensures that even if someone splits the line, they will land on their feet, avoiding dramatic tumbles and painful crotch-to-line collisions!

*Your slackline should look
like this, flat with no tilt, giving you the
most possible surface area on which to balance.*
PATRICK RIFFEL

anchor materials on the far end of the line until there is enough tension in the system to secure them.

Tensioning changes the shape of the slackline, changing the angle to make an increasingly shallow V as more tension is added. You'll know that your line needs more tension if it's bottoming out. A line that touches the ground when weighted in the middle is under-tensioned and needs tension added to make the line walkable. If you plan on adding lots of tension to the system, it's possible to rig your anchors much lower to the ground; this is a great way to rig safe lines for children.

In general tighter lines are more stable than looser ones, and tight lines are best for beginners and dynamic tricks. Low-tension lines feel much different than super tight lines; they are great for slackline yoga and static poses. You can think of tension as the difference between a new trampoline and an old one. New trampolines with tight springs have the potential to launch you high in the air, and you can run across a new trampoline easily. An old trampoline with worn-out springs is like a slackline with low tension: It's a slog to walk across, and everything moves slower, making it tough to catch big air. Forgive the metaphors, but tension is important and something you really need to feel to understand. Experiment with your line as you add

tension. Get it to the point where it's just barely tight enough to avoid bottoming out and try walking it loose, then gradually add tension, testing the line between pulls to see how it feels.

OVER-TENSIONING

Over-tensioning a slackline can result in anchor damage, jammed ratchets, and broken slacklines. Destroying anchors and gear is not only costly but also dangerous. It's easy to avoid over-tensioning by taking breaks during tensioning to feel the line. You will notice when it gets very tight; the webbing will start to feel stiff, and mounting and walking the line will feel different. If you flick a very tight line, it makes a high-pitched noise. When your flick-test sounds loud and the line feels stiff, stop tensioning.

It's easier to over-tension with a ratchet or chain hoist than it is with any type of pulley system. The power of mechanical tensioning systems can cause you to miss the signs of over-tensioning and lead to damaged anchors and gear. Keep your eyes and ears open while tensioning. Listen for cracking in the gear or anchors; watch for movement around the anchor to indicate root displacement. If you see your anchor moving or hear creaks and cracks, the anchor is not safe to use.

There is no excuse for breaking anchors. Don't rush through tensioning. Have a friend watch for

This slackline-specific pulley kit is fully tensioned.

movement or sound on the opposite side to safeguard that anchor too. Choose anchors that do not move when you try to shake them. Never trust any man-made anchor point (like a railing or diving board) outright. Most importantly, never try to tension from a tree smaller in diameter than your thigh.

BACKING UP

Backing up means rigging a fail-safe for any parts of the system that are likely to slip, break, or untie. Think ahead about what would happen if any given piece of your slackline failed; identify parts of your system that are most likely to fail and back them up. For low-consequence lines the tensioning system is often backed up to prevent accidental release.

Backing up the tensioning hardware before pulling the line tight protects the tensioners from a system failure as they pull tension. The slackliners involved in tensioning are in a dangerous position, as they must stand very close to the tensioning hardware. Protect the tensioners by securing a secondary anchor sling to the ratchet or to the line locker side of the pulleys. This ensures that, should any part

Tie the tail of your slackline to the anchor as shown.

of the system fail while tensioning, the tensioning hardware will remain anchored to the tree instead of flying toward the tensioners' faces.

Backing up the tensioning hardware after the line is tight protects walking slackliners from an accidental release of tension during the slackline session. This is standard practice for all types of slacklines, big and small. To back up the tensioning system, take the end of the slackline where it exits the line locker or ratchet and connect it to the anchor. Backing up the tail of the slackline ensures that, should the system lose tension unexpectedly, the slackline will lose only a fraction of its total tension, and all gear will remain in place.

DE-TENSIONING

De-tensioning releases all the stored energy of a slackline in a single move. Rope and webbing can move extremely fast during this stage of rigging. Never de-tension a line as it is being walked; all

slackliners and spectators should stand clear of the slackline and anchors during de-tensioning.

As you de-tension, make sure your hands and body are well away from the pulley system. Extra rope, webbing, or anchor materials may be scattered on the ground near your feet. It's difficult to determine at a glance whether or not any of these materials are linked to the tensioning system; if they are, these materials can wrap around your foot or body and cause injury. Double-check to make sure you, and any spectators, are well clear of all slackline materials.

Rigging a Gibbon Slackline

Building anchors and tensioning systems are the most complex parts of slackline rigging. The ratcheting slackline kit pioneered by brothers Robert and Jan Kaeding of Gibbon Slacklines eliminates the need for either of these tasks. Designed to bring

Gibbon slacklines are popular due to their simple setup.

slacklining to non-climbers, simplified kits like the ones offered by Gibbon can be rigged without any climbing gear or anchor-building know-how. Anchor slings are integrated into the design of the ratchet and slackline, eliminating the need for connecting hardware like line lockers, carabiners, or shackles. The two-piece system consists of a ratchet on one side and 2-inch nylon webbing on the other. Each piece has a loop that can be used as a very basic anchor sling for trees or other primary anchors. The ratchet is a one-piece, hand-crank tensioning device that makes it relatively easy for a single person to tension the line.

Ratcheting slackline kits are limited in their usefulness. More advanced athletes will need to develop some knowledge of climbing gear in order to build a wider variety of lines, but slackline kits are a good way to learn the basics of slackline rigging without delving into serious anchor building or gear selection.

Children as young as 5 can learn how to balance on their own.
FRANKIE NAJERA

Gear

- Slackline kit
- Tree protection
- Two solid primary anchors

Anchors

Protect each anchor with padding to extend the life of your gear and prevent damage to trees. Then use the sewn loops to girth-hitch each end around a primary anchor. Wrap the looped end of each piece around the anchor, running the long end through

This line is not flat; rig yours with a loop and fold to correct the angle of the webbing.
FRANKIE NAJERA

Rig your ratchet so that it hangs below the line. This prevents the weight of the ratchet from tilting the webbing or affecting the dynamics of the slackline.

the sewn loop to make a girth hitch. The slackline should be rigged patterned side up. The rubberized print adds traction to the line; it works especially well when slackliners are wearing shoes.

THE LOOP AND FOLD: KEEPING YOUR LINE FLAT

The loop and fold method can be used to keep the line and ratchet oriented correctly. To keep the slackline flat, fold the webbing in half where it exits the sewn loop. Do this on both anchors. For extra security, fold the line in half all the way around the tree, so that even if your anchor slips slightly, the orientation of the gear won't change.

If your line still seems tilted, the weight of your ratchet might be pulling it sideways. To prevent this, rig so that your ratchet hangs under the line.

The Loop and Fold Step-by-Step

A good slackline is flat. If you're having trouble keeping it that way, you might not be doing the loop and fold correctly.

1. Fold the line carefully in half as it goes through the sewn loop. The better this fold, the flatter your line will be.

2. Extend the fold in the webbing farther around the tree to keep your fold from slipping as tension pulls the line through the loop.

The Loop and Fold: Steps 1 and 2
FRANKIE NAJERA

EXTENDING YOUR RATCHET STRAP

Sometimes the best trees are too big around to fit the ratchet strap. If this is the case, use a loop of webbing, rope, or a climbing sling to add length to the anchor. Link the extra sling to the sewn loop on the anchor using a girth hitch.

An anchor extended with a rope girth-hitched around the sewn loop
HAYLEY ASHBURN

SHORTENING YOUR RATCHET STRAP

If your ratchet is more than a few feet out in the line, its weight can affect the dynamics of the line. To shorten the ratchet strap, wrap it around the anchor two or three times before passing the sewn loop over the ratchet. You can bypass the ratchet sling entirely by clipping a carabiner through the sewn loop where it connects to the ratchet. Clip this carabiner to an anchor sling of your choice. Use caution with this method—the sling is weaker in this configuration because the stitching here isn't reinforced.

Tensioning Correctly with a Ratchet

The ratchet works by slowly turning a bolt, pulling the line tight as it wraps around the bolt's circumference; only a limited amount of webbing can be sucked into the ratchet before the bolt gets full. Piling too much webbing onto the bolt can jam the ratchet, making it difficult to release at the end of the day. To tension your line properly, slide the end of the walking webbing through the bolt in the ratchet and pull out all the slack you can (really pull it hard) before you begin cranking with the ratchet. Hold the line tight as you begin tensioning; don't

An anchor rigged with an independent anchor sling
FRANKIE NAJERA

This is what your line should look like before tensioning: pulled tight, up and off the ground.

crank your ratchet while the line is still loose. After one or two cranks, the webbing will "catch" and the ratchet will hold the webbing on its own.

Over-tensioning with your ratchet can cause it to jam. Over-tensioning usually results from piling up too much webbing on the bolt. Keep an eye on the amount of webbing in your ratchet. You should always be able to see the teeth of the ratchet above the webbing.

If it looks like there's too much webbing on the bolt but your slackline isn't the tension you would like, you probably started cranking a loose line. Release tension, open the ratchet, and start over.

Another way you can jam the ratchet during the tensioning step is by feeding the webbing into the ratchet crooked. Your ratchet sucks up two pieces of webbing as you crank: the slackline and the tail of the slackline. The slackline will usually feed in straight on its own, but the tail has a tendency to

Buck Ashburn cranks his line, feeding the webbing carefully into the ratchet with one hand.

This ratchet has too much webbing on the bolt.

This ratchet is properly loaded; the teeth are clearly visible above the webbing on both sides of the bolt.

This webbing is about to jam the ratchet. If your webbing looks like this, release tension and start over.

If the line is feeding into the ratchet crooked, pull the ratchet in the opposite direction to change the angle of feed.

Crank with your front hand and hold the tail of the line straight with your other.

feed into the ratchet crooked. Keep an eye on the tail; you may need to hold it in place to ensure that the webbing is lined up correctly while tensioning.

SOLO MISSION: TENSIONING BY YOURSELF

I set up slacklines by myself all the time, and after a while not only do my hands get sore, but it also gets difficult to crank the ratchet. To protect your hands, and get some extra leverage, use the tail of your slackline to extend the handle.

1. Wrap a loop at the very end of the tail around the ratchet handle, leaving plenty of webbing to feed into the ratchet.
2. Get underneath the line and use your feet for leverage.

Frankie Najera on a solo mission
FRANKIE NAJERA

Backing Up the System

If you are using a ratchet, the built-in lock is a backup. Always remember to lock the ratchet before you start walking, so that the line won't lose tension unexpectedly. This is especially important if you are slacklining with children who might play with the ratchet, or if slackliners mounting the line will be stepping on the ratchet.

To lock a ratchet, push the handle down and back toward the anchor as far as it will go. Pull back on the brake bar; the ratchet handle will squeeze down an additional centimeter or two. Release the

You can tell this ratchet is locked because the bottom bar rests inside the notch.

HAYLEY ASHBURN

For extra backup, wrap the hanging tail of the slackline around the anchor and tie a bowline. If there's not enough tail, use a sling, rope, or piece of webbing scrap.

Backing up the ratchet on a longer slackline

brake after the ratchet is completely closed. The ratchet locks by securing the brake bar in a notch behind the teeth.

If your slackline is longer than average, there may be no tail left hanging after tensioning. To back up the ratchet in this case, thread a piece of webbing or cord through the ratchet and secure to the primary anchor.

De-tensioning

To release tension with a ratchet, pull the gold bar back to disengage the lock and open the ratchet as far as possible. The ratchet will make a loud cracking sound and release. If the ratchet doesn't release easily, apply more pressure to the handle and it should open.

You can gain some distance between yourself and the ratchet by using the tail of the webbing. Open the ratchet as far as possible and thread the end of the tail through the lock handle. Pull the lock open with the tail, then kick the ratchet open.

To release a jammed ratchet, insert any tool that will fit and depress the gold bar; this will release the brake.
HAYLEY ASHBURN

De-tensioning a trickline
FRANKIE NAJERA

Building an Aid

If you or your friends are having trouble getting stable, try building a learning aid. Fasten a rope from one anchor to the other at head height above the line. When placed within easy reach, a guideline provides a third point of contact to keep beginners from falling.

You can make a learning aid kid-friendly by using a small rope to rig a handle at kid-height. Attach a length of rope to the aid using a carabiner. The carabiner will slide along and kids can jump around without an adult holding their hand.

Warning: Rig your aid carefully from branches strong enough to hold the weight of an adult. Test the aid to make sure it can hold your full weight before using it as a handle.

The Spider Web

The popularity of slacklining is due in large part to the appeal of belonging to a fun slackline community. When Gibbon Slacklines opened their US branch, they sent me and a few other slackliners around the country to teach slacklining and host exciting community slackline events. We threw slackline parties for people of all ages to spread awareness of the sport and show beginners how much fun slacklining can be. One of the things people liked best was our slackline spider web. The spider web is a three-way, multi-person slackline matrix that can turn any slackline session into a high-energy group activity. On a spider web, multiple slackers can race to the middle, or compete for who can balance the longest, simultaneously balance, learn to walk, or be playful on the line.

A slackline spider web
FRANKIE NAJERA

All you need is a pair of slackline kits to build the spider web and three equally spaced trees or other anchors. One slackline is anchored as normal to two trees. The second slackline is anchored to the center of the first and then to the remaining tree. To anchor one slackline to another, thread the sewn loop of a second slackline onto the first *before* tensioning. Then anchor the ratchet side of the second line to the third tree and crank it tight. As tension on the second line increases, its sewn loop will pull the first slackline back like a slingshot, bending the first line in the middle to create a V shape. The result is three semi-independent lines that bounce together and lend themselves to the less skilled antics of kids. Beginners will love standing in the middle where it's easy to balance with a foot on each line. Spider webs are great for parties because three or more kids (or adults) can walk the lines simultaneously.

HOW TO RIG THE SLACKLINE SPIDER WEB

You will need three good primary anchors spaced at approximately equal distances from one another and two slackline kits. The kits will be called slackline A and B for clarity.

1. Anchor the webbing side of slackline A to any of the three trees.
2. Thread the webbing tail of slackline A through the sewn loop of slackline B.
3. Anchor a ratchet to one of the other two trees.
4. Thread the end of slackline A through the ratchet, positioning the sewn loop of line B in the middle of slackline A.
5. Pull out as much slack from slackline A as possible and crank the ratchet just enough to secure the webbing. You will come back and tension this one more later, so leave room on the bolt for more webbing.
6. Adjust the sewn loop of slackline B so it is centered on slackline A.
7. Crank tension on slackline B with the ratchet anchored to the third tree. The webbing of slackline A should bend toward the center of all three trees, like a Mercedes logo.
8. Adjust tension on both lines to modify the shape of your spider web. The web is more fun when rigged tightly.
9. Make sure both ratchets are locked, and let the fun begin!

Simple Slackline Anchors

All beginner slacklines are built with simple anchors. A simple anchor uses one primary anchor point, usually a tree, to anchor the slackline. The sling clips to the slackline at the master point. Always use a locking carabiner at the master point for extra security.

Constructing Anchor Slings

After the primary anchor point is wrapped for protection, it can be slung in a number of ways with webbing, static rope, or spansets. The anchor should be the strongest part of your slackline system. If the anchor fails, hardware is likely to come free, moving very fast in the direction of the opposite anchor. For this reason webbing and aluminum carabiners must be used with caution. For longline anchors, always use spansets or static rope and shackles or steel carabiners.

THE GIRTH-HITCH METHOD

If your sling is long enough, try girth-hitching it around the entire anchor point. A girth-hitch anchor, once set, stays in place during rigging, while a slung anchor will fall to the ground unless it is under tension. Girth-hitch your anchor slings to hold protection in place or secure slings in the correct spot.

THE BASKET METHOD

For the basket method a continuous loop of material is folded in half and two bights are used for the master point. Webbing has the most holding power

Bad slackline anchors can be dangerous and against park or city rules.

when rigged in a loop, such as in the basket. Wrap a sling around the anchor point and clip both ends with a carabiner to create this anchor. The basket is a good enough anchor for low-consequence lines, but the carabiner will always be slightly tri-loaded.

THE LOOPED-END METHOD

Materials like static rope can be rigged in a single strand with looped ends. These anchors are convenient if you have static rope on hand, and can be adjusted to fit a variety of anchor sizes. To rig a looped-end anchor, tie two loops onto the ends of a rope and clip the loops together to make a master point.

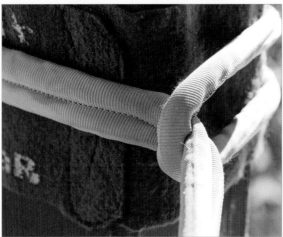

The three most common sling configurations for simple slackline anchors. Top to bottom: looped ends, girth hitch, basket style.

The Master Point

The master point is where the slackline clips to the anchor sling, usually with a locking carabiner, though shackles, rappel rings, and quick links work here too. The angle and location of the master point can cause your line to tilt sideways, or can even break a carabiner. To correct for angle, orient your master point so the connecting hardware lies flat and the webbing clips to the master point with the walking side of the webbing facing up.

The hardware at the master point holds the most force of any other single piece of gear in the slackline system. Make sure that all master point carabiners are completely closed, and watch out for tri-loading. A carabiner is designed to hold two objects pulling along the biner's longest axis only; pulling against the gate or any other part of the carabiner is unsafe. This three-way pulling commonly happens at slackline master points where biners are used to connect three points: each end of the sling and the line locker. The hardware at the master point can get tri-loaded, meaning there are three directions of pull on the biner, rather than the two it was designed for. To prevent tri-loading your hardware, position the master point at least a foot away from the tree. The two arms of the anchor should be at a 45-degree angle or less. Any wider an angle and your anchor will pull the hardware along its short axis and overly stress the sling.

A well-rigged master point: The carabiner lies flat and the slings are not significantly tri-loading the biner.

A tri-loaded carabiner: This master point was rigged too close to the tree.

Thread a second sling through the first for a quick way to move the master point away from the tree.

On this basic anchor made from climbing slings, the master point is rigged at a good, safe distance from the post because the angle between the two arms of the sling is around 45 degrees.

Webbing Anchors

Webbing makes a good anchor for small, low-tension slacklines, but is not strong enough for long-line or highline anchors. Inspect webbing anchors regularly for nicks and burn marks. If the webbing becomes stiff or faded, think about retiring it.

Webbing is strongest when doubled and used as a sling in a basket formation. Nearly all slackline anchors are rigged from some sort of sling. You can buy pre-sewn climbing slings or make your own slings from bulk webbing.

PRE-SEWN CLIMBING SLINGS

They might look skinny, but climbing slings are a super light and strong way to hold a slackline to its anchors. Plus, since a hitch is used to connect them and adjust the length, there's no knot to worry about untying. The average climbing sling is only a couple of feet long. You'll usually need to connect several together in order to get around a tree; a girth hitch is the fastest way to extend your sling without tying a knot.

Rigging a Pre-sewn Climbing Sling

1. Run one sling through the middle of another.
2. Run one end of the first sling through itself again and pull.
3. Attach several slings in a row like this to make a longer sling.
4. Clip the ends together with a carabiner and link to your slackline.

MAKING YOUR OWN SLINGS

Making your own slings using 1-inch climbing webbing is easier and cheaper than buying pre-sewn slings. Use a water knot to connect both ends of your webbing into a sling, but remember that these knots will be very difficult to untie once you've used them on a slackline. You should consider them permanent. Make your slings on the long side to accommodate a wide range of tree sizes. These slings are good for any tricklining or lowlining purposes, but water knots weaken webbing slightly, so custom-rigged webbing slings are

A finished girth hitch should look like this.

not a good choice for longline or highline anchors. I find 1-inch tubular nylon holds water knots and hitches better than any other type of webbing. Watch out when using flat webbings for any type of rigging involving knots because they have a tendency to slip.

To make a sling from bulk webbing, tie both ends of the webbing together with a water knot to make a continuous loop. Leave at least 3 inches of tail on each side.

ADJUSTABLE WEBBING ANCHORS

To make an adjustable sling, use an untied piece of tubular webbing, a locking carabiner, and a steel ring. The ring on the master point of this anchor will make your slackline lie perfectly flat, and the hitch on the biner is easy to remove, even after holding tension. You can tie the adjustable webbing

anchor over and over again to accommodate a variety of primary anchor points.

Rigging an Adjustable Webbing Anchor

1. Fold a piece of webbing in half and bring both ends together.
2. Use both ends to tie a double girth hitch with a bight release around the carabiner.
3. You just made a big loop; slip a ring onto the loop.
4. Clip the loop with your biner to make a doubled sling as shown.

Spanset Anchors

Spansets are the strongest of all slackline anchor slings. Rated to hold up to 10,000 pounds, spansets may be overkill for your backyard trickline, but you can depend on them to last much longer than any

An adjustable webbing anchor is considered by the author to be the perfect anchor because it completely eliminates the possibility of triloading a carabiner.

Wrap a spanset around the anchor in a basket formation and clip with a carabiner or shackle.

Girth-hitch a spanset for an anchor that won't slip down before tensioning.

other anchor sling. Available in lengths from 2 feet to more than 12 feet, spansets make exceptional anchors because of their strength and durability. The outside sheath of a spanset is extremely abrasion resistant, making this sling a great buy for longliners and aspiring highliners. The bulkiness of spansets also provides extra padding between the anchor and the tree.

Static Rope Anchors

Anchors made from rope are much stronger than webbing anchors, and there's no need to tie your rope in a sling, because a single strand of good static rope tied in the looped-end configuration is more than strong enough for a longline or highline anchor. It's easier to tie and untie knots in static rope compared to webbing anchors, so you can use the same length of static rope over and over again to tie anchors of all sizes. Rig static rope in a looped-end configuration by tying loops at each end with figure eight knots. You'll need 9 or more feet of static rope, rated for climbing or rescue use, with a diameter of at least 8 millimeters.

Rigging a Static Rope Anchor

1. Double over one end of the rope to make a bight.
2. Tie a figure eight knot on a bight, leaving at least 6 inches of tail.
3. Do this on both sides to make a loop at each end.
4. Clip both loops with a carabiner for the master point.

Knots can be difficult to untie once a slackline is tensioned on them. If you plan on rigging a line longer than 100 feet, you might want to consider using a spanset rather than a static rope anchor due to the high forces involved.

A-Framing

The environment doesn't always provide ideal primary anchor points. A-framing can help compensate for anchors that are too weak, too low, or too far apart. The name *A-frame* comes from the original design, which was built with two straight pieces of wood bolted together in the shape of an A. You can use anything stable to serve the purpose of an A-frame; a sturdy chair works, and a pile of rocks or a milk crate will do.

These simple structures divert the slackline by creating a high point for the webbing to rest on. The A-frame acts like an intermediary anchor, absorbing some of the slackline's force and changing the direction of pull on the primary anchor point. Because the line pulls on the base rather than the middle of the primary anchor point, it puts less stress on the anchor as a whole. This is a great way

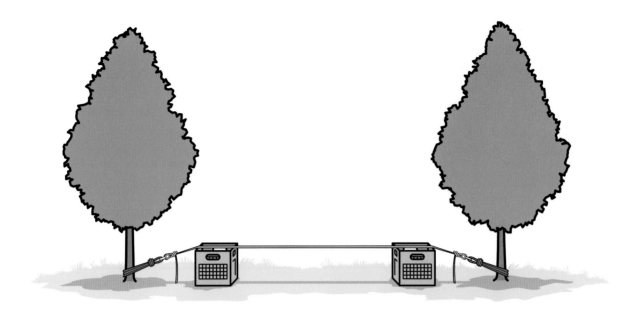

Use A-frames to turn questionable anchors into solid anchors.

to rig from smaller trees or urban objects like telephone poles and light posts.

Build your simple anchor just as you would for any other slackline, but rather than positioning it at the desired height of your line, slide the anchor all the way to the base of the anchor object. The line needs to come *up* and over the A-frame to achieve stability. The master point of your anchor should be lower than the top of your A-frame by at least 6 inches.

If you'd like to rig a line that is shorter than the space between your anchors, put an A-frame in the middle, or put an A-frame at each end of your desired line. The line will act and feel as if it were rigged from the A-frames rather than the far anchors.

A slackline A-framed over a stump

Ground Anchors

The ground anchor is a technique borrowed from canyoneering. When a canyoneer needs to rappel down into a canyon, and there is nothing to tie his rope to, he buries a rock in the sand to make what canyoneers call a dead-man anchor. Slackliners can combine this technique with a pair of A-frames to build simple anchors when trees are in short supply.

The ground anchor is a great way to build a slackline on the beach, in the desert, or anywhere without big trees. These anchors can last an afternoon, or a lifetime, and there's nothing to uninstall when de-rigging a ground anchor. Simply cut the anchor sling where it emerges from the ground; the wooden stakes should degrade on their own. It does take a considerable amount of time and commitment to dig a strong ground anchor. The depth of the hole depends on the hardness of the ground; soft mediums like sand require deeper holes

to get the job done. To make a ground anchor, you will need something to bury; I recommend a thick, 2-foot-long piece of timber or metal, or a thick bundle of wooden stakes. You'll also need an A-frame and an anchor sling or chain.

Rigging a Ground Anchor

1. Cut and roll the grass back if necessary.
2. Dig a hole about 4 feet deep (deeper in sand, shallower in clay—use your judgment).
3. Wrap your anchor sling securely around the stakes and bury them in the hole, lying flat and perpendicular to the direction of your planned slackline.
4. Fill up the hole, stomping down the layers after every few inches and sprinkling water to pack it down. You don't want to make a mud pit, but a little moisture will cement your anchor in the earth.

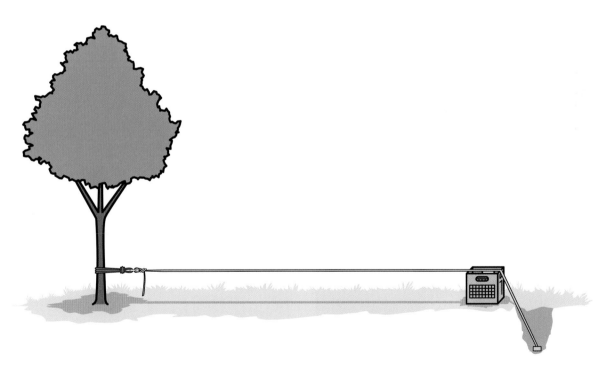

The anchor sling on a ground anchor comes out of the ground at a slight diagonal.

5. Wait 24 hours for the earth to settle and dry. This part is very important. Nothing is worse than digging a whole anchor only to have it pull out of the ground because you were impatient.
6. Position an A-frame about 3 feet from the anchor.
7. Attach your line and tension it, watching for movement in the ground. If the ground moves, the line will probably need to sit longer or be re-dug.

Rigging a Primitive Line

Rigging a primitive line is the first step to learning advanced rigging techniques. Even if you have fancy, slackline-specific gear, it's worth learning how to rig

a primitive line, because the principles you learn here are repeated throughout all slackline rigging.

There are a few ways to rig a primitive line. The technique here is called the Ellington pulley system, which is a simple way to tension your slackline using carabiners. The gear for this line is classic climbing gear that has been around for decades and should be available wherever climbing equipment is sold.

Gear

- Four or five oval climbing carabiners
- One 1-inch rappel ring
- Two slings or lengths of rope
- At least 50 feet of 1-inch webbing

Step 1: The Static End

Choose a solid primary anchor point, and test and pad the anchor before building an anchor sling. Wrap the anchor with a climbing sling, rope, or spanset and connect both ends of the sling with a single carabiner. This will be your master point.

Primitive lines like this one are perfect for the backyard or the park.

Primitive slacklines require minimal gear and use the webbing itself to apply tension.

An anchor built with a climbing sling for the static end of a primitive line

TYING THE LINE LOCKER HITCH

The next step is building a line locker to link the webbing to the master point. For the line locker on the static end, I like to tie a line locker hitch right onto the master point carabiner. This hitch uses no extra gear, holds the line flat without damaging it, and is easy to release when you're ready to de-rig. If someone forgets to pack their rings, you can save the day by improvising this line locker using no more than a single carabiner. It's good for small tricklines, primitive lines, and low-tension lines. It is not safe to rig on highlines or high-tension lines.

I like to use an oval, non-locking carabiner for all parts of a primitive line, because the oval shape and smooth edges accommodate 1-inch webbing without folding or creasing the material. However, any carabiner will work.

An oval carabiner (top) and a wire-gate carabiner (bottom)

1. Hold your webbing walking side up (the printed side showing) and thread the tail down through the biner and back toward yourself.

Step 1

2. Pull the tail tight and fold it over the walking end to the right. All pieces should lie walking side up.

Step 2

3. Bring the tail around behind the right edge of the biner and push a bight through the center.

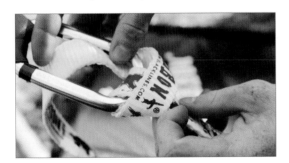

Step 3

4. Push the bight through the loop you made in step 3.

Step 4

5. Pull firmly on the slackline to set the knot.

Step 5

6. The bight should look inside out, and the rest of the hitch should be walking side up.

To untie this line locker, pull firmly on the hanging tail in the direction of the tree. The bight should slide out easily. Leave more tail hanging out of the bight to make this step easier.

Once your webbing is hitched onto the anchor, you've finished rigging the static end of the slackline. To begin building the dynamic end, run your webbing across to the other anchor and lay it out on the ground, walking side up. It's important to make sure that your next line locker is rigged on the right side of the webbing. Keep track of which side is "up" so that there are no twists in the finished slackline.

Step 2: The Dynamic End

The dynamic end will have your Ellington primitive pulley system on it. This is the end you will pull from.

For this end, clip two non-locking oval carabiners to the anchor sling. The gates of the biners should open the same way. This will help you thread long pieces of webbing through later.

You'll need to build a basic line locker with a rappel ring and carabiner for this end of the slack-

The master point of the dynamic end; colored carabiners are used here for clarity.

line. The line locker should be placed some distance from the anchor slings; you will pull this distance out of the slackline with the primitive tensioning system. The distance between the line locker and the anchor varies depending on the length of the slackline. Leave one-fifth the total length of the gap between the line locker and dynamic end anchor. Nylon webbing walks best between 15–20 percent

stretch, so you'll have to remove that much from the line through the tensioning process so that the line doesn't touch the ground while you're in the middle.

BUILDING A BASIC LINE LOCKER

The line locker is a foundational slacklining concept; line lockers link webbing to the system without compromising the strength of the material or damaging the webbing. You should always treat your webbing with extreme care. The webbing is generally the least durable piece of gear in the system. Unlike rope that has a sheath over its core, webbing has no sheath, and its flattened shape gives it a high ratio of surface area to volume. Basically, even though it has great strength, webbing is kind of delicate. For this reason riggers are very careful about how their webbing is anchored to the system.

Line lockers are designed to hold webbing flat under high tension without damaging the material or cinching tight like a knot. Webbing can easily get "nicks," or small cuts, where it attaches to the anchor, and once a slackline is tensioned, a knot in the webbing is almost impossible to untie without damaging the nylon. Line lockers are friction-based anchors that hold the webbing without nicking it, and slide out of the system easily when tension on the slackline is released. The basic line locker can be used on anything from beginner slacklines to serious highlines.

You'll need a single 1-inch ring, aluminum or steel, preferably continuous with a smooth edge rather than a welded seam.

1. Pull a bight through the ring.

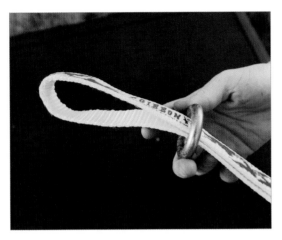

Step 1

2. Fold the bight over onto the tail side of the webbing to form a circle like a snake biting its own tail.

Step 2

3. Slide the ring over the end of the bight.

Step 3

4. Clip a carabiner through the head of the bight, around all three strands of webbing. The biner should lie on the anchor side of the slackline.

Step 4

5. Pull the tails away from the carabiner to set and finish.

Step 5

Step 3: Tensioning with the Ellington

You will use the excess webbing hanging from the tail of the line locker to build an Ellington for tensioning. The Ellington uses carabiners to create a primitive pulley system, giving you a small mechanical advantage for tensioning your line. Where a real pulley system would use rope, you will be using the tail, or excess, of your slackline. It is essential to keep all your webbing entirely flat for this whole process. If there is a twist anywhere in your Ellington, start over, because something has gone wrong.

If you refer to the photo sequence, you can see that the Ellington is very similar to a simple spiral. This is the exact path your webbing will follow: Points 1 and 3 are on the master point of your slackline anchor. Points 2 and 4 will be rigged onto the carabiner side of the line locker. The actual system will be condensed; the strands of webbing will come close to touching, but the line does not actually cross itself at any point.

Point 4 represents a friction lock, which is the brake of your system. Two pieces of webbing share a carabiner here, with point 4 lying underneath point 2; the friction created by tension prevents them from slipping past one another.

RIGGING THE ELLINGTON TENSIONING SYSTEM

1. Pull the tail of webbing hanging on the anchor side of the line locker.

Step 1

2. Thread the tail up through the bottom carabiner on the master point and back toward the line locker.

Step 2

3. Thread the tail up through the line locker biner and back in the other direction. This is point 2.

Step 3

4. This step is the only one in which you will thread the webbing down and through the carabiner. Run the webbing to the master point and thread it down and through the topmost biner.

Step 4

The master point should look like this.

5. To make the friction lock at point 4, thread the webbing up through the biner so that it fits entirely and neatly underneath the webbing already on the biner.

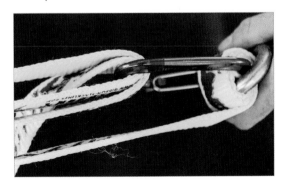

Step 5

6. Pull the tail straight toward the dynamic anchor to tension the slackline.

Step 6

To de-rig your slackline, simply pull the tail away from the friction lock to disengage the two pieces of webbing.

De-rigging the Ellington

Rigging a Slackline-Specific Pulley Kit

The Slackline Brothers pulley system is the only slackline-specific pulley kit currently available. Because they're designed for slacklining, SBI pulleys are the simplest to use and a good introduction to pulley rigging. The rope comes pre-threaded through the system, and the brake and pulleys are designed to clip directly to your weblock and master point. Because they are less expensive than most other pulley systems, you'll sacrifice some efficiency, and the pulleys have an upper length limit of around 400 feet. The set is steel, so it is heavy but durable, and all the pieces are replaceable. SBIs are a workhorse pulley—they can be used and abused, and relied on to rig moderate slacklines, longlines, and even highlines.

Gear

Slackline Brothers pulley kit including:

- Webbing
- Two line lockers
- Two locking carabiners
- Anchor slings
- Tree protection
- Multiplier

Step 1: The Static End

Rig the static end anchor and clip the master point to a line locker at one end of the webbing. See page

Pulley kits are perfect for any level of slackliner.

Everything needed to rig a slackline pulley kit

60 (Rigging a Primitive Line) for the step-by-step breakdown on rigging a basic line locker.

Step 2: The Dynamic End

Walk the webbing over to the dynamic end, laying it out flat with no twists on the ground between the two anchors. The pulley system will stretch the end of your webbing closer to the dynamic anchor as it tensions the slackline. You will need to position the line locker some distance from the anchor in order to account for the movement of the pulleys. However, if you place the line locker too far from the tree, your pulleys will stretch too far out into what should be the walking line; place the line locker too close, and you won't have enough room to sufficiently tension your slackline. To determine the correct location of the line locker, estimate the total distance between both anchors and divide by five. Tie your line locker that distance from the dynamic end.

Step 3: Tensioning with Slackline Pulleys

SBI pulleys have two sides: one with a brake and one without a brake. Clip the end with the brake to the master point of your anchor; the brake arm should hang down below the master point.

Rigging the brake end of the pulleys to a shackle on the master point of the dynamic end anchor

You might need to untwist the pulley rope for this next step. To do so, grab both ropes coming out the top of the braking pulley block, one in each hand, and walk slowly backwards until you reach the other pulley block. Now it should be easy to position the second block correctly.

A. *Use the ropes coming out of the anchored pulley as a guide to untwist your ropes.*

B. *Twisted pulley ropes*

C. *Correctly aligned pulley ropes*

Have a friend hold the brake arm down to allow the pulleys to extend; you may need to manually feed rope into the pulleys at this point.

Pushing this arm upward disengages the brake, allowing my partner to extend the pulleys.

Extend the pulleys and clip to the line locker with a locking carabiner.

Stretch the pulleys as far as necessary to clip the block to your line locker.

Pull rope out of the pulley system until the line reaches your desired tension. The more people pulling on the rope together, the easier this step will be. People power is awesome! Never hesitate to ask for help in the park.

Pulling tension before adding multipliers

Step 4: Building a Multiplier

A multiplier is a rope-grabbing device such as a prusik, tibloc, or ropeman (shown below) plus one carabiner and one single pulley. There are many options to choose from when building a multiplier, but they all end up doing the same thing: increasing your ability to pull tension.

For lines 100 feet and under, a single multiplier is sufficient on the SBI system. For lines anywhere from 120 to 400 feet, you will want two multipliers. (Prepare to spend quite some time and energy tensioning a 400-foot line if you are solo.)

A line rigged with double multipliers

1. To build your multiplier, locate the strand of rope running through the brake arm (this is the strand you used to pull). This strand should be tensioned behind the brake and un-tensioned on the other side. Place the tibloc on the tensioned strand so that the narrow end points toward the brake arm.

Follow the rope through the brake; the piece on top is the one you want.

2. Clip a carabiner through the hole in the tibloc.

After positioning the tibloc on the correct rope, clip a carabiner through the hole and slide it to the thin end of the tibloc, camming the rope against the tibloc's teeth.

3. Grab the tail of the pulley rope and insert it into your single pulley.

Loading the single pulley with static rope

4. Clip the pulley to the tibloc.

A completed multiplier

5. Slide the tibloc as far as possible away from the brake arm and resume pulling your slackline tight; it should feel considerably easier.

The multiplier will move closer to the brake as you pull rope through the system. When the multiplier reaches the braking pulley block, slide it back to the other end and resume pulling. The multiplier only slides in one direction.

If pulling does not feel easier, you may have rigged your tibloc on the wrong strand of rope; go back and correct it. The tibloc will move toward the brake arm as you tension; when it reaches the brake, simply stop pulling, slide it back in the direction it came, and resume pulling.

OVER-TENSIONING

Something to be aware of with SBI pulleys is that the brake starts slipping at around 3,000 pounds. It is impossible to drastically over-tension SBI pulleys because the brake will not hold more than that. If you do indeed tension too much, the rope will make a funny noise and slide back through slowly until the line reaches 3,000 pounds tension. Let some rope out and the brake will catch and stop slipping.

Usually the brake slips no more than a few inches, and it happens directly after you finish a round of tensioning. The rope should never slip after the brake has already caught. If the brake stops working well, it means the teeth are wearing down and you will need to replace the brake. Expect to replace your brake after a couple of years of heavy use. Replacement brakes are available through Slackline Brothers, and it can be done easily at home.

Step 5: Backing Up

Protect yourself from slippage by tying an overhand knot close behind the brake after tensioning. Or tie off the end of the pulley rope to a knot on the master point of the anchor.

A basic stopper-action backup knot

Tying off the end of the pulley ropes to create a backup

Step 6: De-tensioning

Once your line is rigged and you've played, you have two options for how to de-tension your line. The first option is to just "kick" the integrated brake forward and let the rope fly though the brake.

Kicking the brake arm—the pulley rope will fly a little!

Positioning the biners for a Z-release

This is the easiest method, but can be dangerous at high tension (100-plus feet). At lower tensions, kicking the brake forward is a completely acceptable method of de-tensioning. Just be rope aware, and keep in mind the direction the rope is going to be flying; make sure it has room to fly, and that no

one is in the way (especially you). Face away from the brake as you kick it. The brake will catch the rope again, so you may have to kick it forward two or three times before your line is fully de-tensioned.

The second method is the "Z there and back release," for which you'll need two carabiners

Redirecting the pulley rope into a Z-shape

Releasing tension using the Z there and back release method

(thin-profile sport climbing biners are best). Clip one carabiner through the hole in the end of the brake. Clip another through the master point. Now you have two carabiners dangling from opposite sides of the pulleys.

Take the tail of rope coming through the brake and clip it to the far carabiner. After you go "there" and clip it, then take the rope "back" to the brake and clip it through the carabiner clipped in the eyelet, making a Z-shape.

From there you can stand and pull your rope, which pulls the carabiner on the brake in the direction that *opens* the brake.

Take a firm grip on the rope, and slowly release the brake by pulling the rope. Once the brake is open, slowly release tension. This is the safest way to release tension on longer lines, because much of the force is negated by friction caused by the Z formation the rope is clipped into.

After you are finished slacklining, you will want to store your SBI pulleys. Pull out rope through the brake, shortening your pulleys until they are about 3 feet long. Place the roped part of the pulleys over your neck, letting the metal casing hang below each shoulder. From the brake, start butterfly coiling the rope over your shoulders, leaving the last 5 feet of rope on the ground. Take the rope and the pulleys off your shoulders, and use your arm to maintain the upside-down U; make sure to not disturb the coils. Take the extra 5 feet of rope and make a few wraps around the upper part of the coil closest to your arm. Make sure to leave enough room for your arm to pull through and out—otherwise you won't be able to remove the coil from your arm! Once you have made a few wraps, pull your arm out, put a bight through the eye of the loop (where your arm was), and open the loop over the head of the coil. This girth-hitches the coil, improving the likelihood that it will remain undisturbed before your next use of the pulleys. Tie off the excess and throw it in the bag; it's time to search for your next line!

Start with the shortened pulleys around your neck.

Butterfly coil the remaining pulley rope.

Secure your pulleys into the butterfly coil.

Competitive Tricklining:
Meet World Champion Andy Lewis

Andy Lewis has always been a little bit off the wall. He was banned from the Natural Games for free soloing (that's walking leashless), lost a sponsorship in 2010 for leaking pictures of a naked high-line walk, and has waged a long battle against the National Park Service over the legality of parachuting in the parks.

Despite all the missteps, Lewis seems to be the first at everything in the slackline world. He landed the first backflip on the line; he won the first slackline World Cup; he was the first slackliner to be featured in a major commercial (for Nike); and his tricklining prowess even earned him a spot

Since 2006, Andy Lewis has been the biggest innovator of the sport.

onstage with Madonna, throwing backflips and butt-bounces during the 2012 Super Bowl half-time show. He is soon to be the first slackliner to star in a feature film. Until recently Lewis held the world record for longest highline ever walked—a 312-foot-long, 400-foot-high slackline in Moab, Utah—a record that has now been broken.

Andy slacklines as easily as he breathes, and his passion for the sport has made him one of the best. He talked with me about pushing the limits of slacklining, and how he came to be such a success.

Q: You've been at the forefront of slacklining for your whole career. You were the first American-sponsored slackliner, and you're a world champion trickliner, a record-holding highliner and longliner. What advice do you have for beginners in the sport?

A: Set up a low, short slackline and try until you can do it. Then set it longer and higher and try until you can do that one and so on. Brenden Gebhart (a trickliner on the Balance Community team) says, "Obsession to progression." I like that a lot.

As far as other tips, I would say try to keep square to the line. You have a box between your shoulders and hips; keep it squared on the anchor and walk straight forward.

Keep good posture in your back. Stand straight up, not leaning back or hunched over. You've gotta learn to work with all the wigglies—to do that, besides staying square, for me it's really all about focus.

Q: What is your preferred slackline for tricklining?

A: A 17- to 19-meter-long Gibbon Surfline with two long-lever ratchets, over grass, about 3.5 feet high.

Q: Why so high?

A: The advantage of rigging it so high is you get lots of power in your line. It's high enough for me to do an atomic butt-bounce or chest-bounce without hitting the ground. At the same time it's low enough where you won't have high-consequence falls. It's a balance between risk and availability of tricks for me.

Q: You've been tricklining since the beginning. How have you seen modern equipment change slacklining during the course of your career?

A: I would say that new gear has changed slacking in three different ways: First, it's changed the cost to get into slacklining. It is now very inexpensive, although if you want, it can be a bottomless pit for investments. Second, more lines are possible now that we have the gear to rig them. Jerry Miszewski, Chris Rigby, and I rigged a 1,250-foot line a few days ago. None of us could walk the thing, but even a couple of years ago it wouldn't have been possible to rig.

And finally, the style of slacklining has been affected. The 2-inch tricklines have totally transformed modern-day tricklining. The wider webbing makes it easier to land tricks that were never even conceived of as plausible before. Having this new gear exposed to a new style of slacker like we're seeing, who's influenced by parkour and skating culture, will lead to progressively more difficult tricks. Right now it's all about bounce, and the Gibbon line is just a really good combination of flexibility and power.

It's really just opened up a whole bunch of crazy movements. The butt-bounce and chest-bounce define slacklining right now, along with

Andy's fire line, rigged with a simple slackline kit and a little white gas. Don't try this at home.
HAYLEY ASHBURN

rotations and flips. The amount of slacklining you can do is just gigantic.

Q: How is it that you are credited with being the first to land so many tricks? From the double drop-knee, to the backflip, to chest-bouncing and back-bouncing, it seems like you've influenced tricklining style more than anyone out there. How did that happen?

A: It's all about time and place. When I landed the first backflip in 2006, no one had done it before; a lot of people couldn't even get their lines off the ground, much less rig them tight enough to do a backflip.

A lot of the tricks I've invented, people were thinking about, but I just did it first. I mean, bouncing off your chest and back had been done on a trampoline before, but on a slackline it was just new. Also, two to three years ago I was one of the only people putting videos on the Internet and sharing what I learned.

People copy my tricks because they're fun, they look cool and challenging, and they make you stronger. Also, they allow you to think about new tricks *you* can land. You've gotta take this stuff and make the style your own.

It's about being creative. I would look at slacklining and say, "I'm only going to try tricks today that I haven't done before. I could do a double drop-knee, but I won't. I'm gonna do a switch double drop-knee." Eventually you feel more comfortable; you learn how to use the power of the line to your advantage. And that comes with time. I put together pieces of style I learned all around the world. I try to develop many styles of tricks—static moves, combos, rotations—trying to complete trickling, show how you can use the line in many different ways.

Q: How do you think slacklining has changed your life?

A: Other than just being physically stronger in every way? My reaction speed is faster. I'm more flexible and powerful. I have more awareness of my body. All those things come with slacklining, but the real difference is the mental focus you gain. When you learn to turn on your focus and control your body, it affects every aspect of your life.

Q: Could you articulate why it's important for slackliners to get involved with their local community?

A: Slacklining by yourself eventually gets old. Friends make slacklining fun; it's a social sport. You can hang out with friends around the slackline and change the environment you're in. Also, people should know that it's an open sport. When you can watch people's videos from across the world and ask questions on blogs, that communication within the community helps inspire evolution and increases the rate at which people learn to slackline. The sport developed and became big on the Internet. I think we're going to see that communication continue to grow exponentially over the next couple of years.

Lewis was the first slackliner ever to land a backflip on a slackline. It seems like an impossible trick, but with a lot of practice and a super tight slackline, anyone can do a backflip dismount.

More Power: Getting the Line Tighter with Andy Lewis

Five-time world champion of tricklining, Andy Lewis pioneered most of the tricks that have become standard for competitive slacklining. Andy's tricklining has made him a celebrity in the slackline world, but you don't have to be a star to appreciate his stellar setup for trickline training.

If you've moved on to jumping and butt-bouncing tricks and want a little more amplitude out of your line, you can use Andy's setup to take your trickline to the next level. Andy builds his with a Gibbon slackline and two Surfline ratchets, creating a line with two dynamic ends.

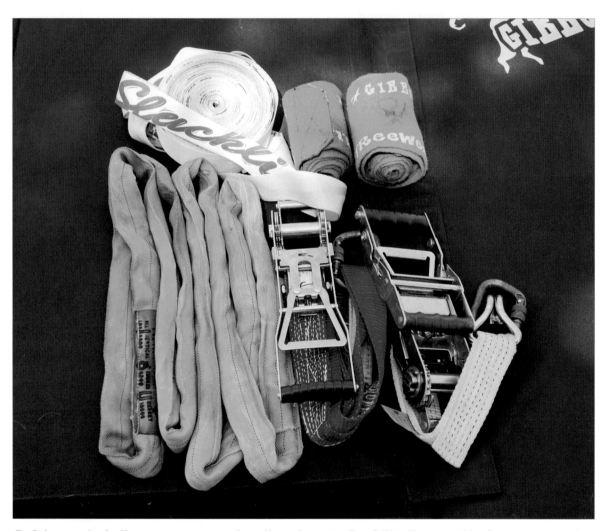

Andy's gear, including two spanset anchor slings for extra durability. You can skip the spansets and simply use the loop and fold method to connect your ratchets to the anchors if you'd rather not spend the cash on spansets.

How to Rig Andy's Trickline Training Line

To build Andy's training line, use any Gibbon slackline kit rigged with two ratchets instead of one.

1. Build your first anchor with the handle of the ratchet hanging below the line.

Step 1

2. Pull the sewn loop of the slackline through the bolt (you will have to work it in slowly) and crank the ratchet one or two clicks, just enough to lock the webbing in place. You will come back to this ratchet and add tension later.

Step 2

3. Anchor the second ratchet to the other side and thread the slackline through, tensioning as much as possible.

Step 3

4. Return to the opposite anchor and add more tension to the first ratchet until it is as tight as you like. Now you have twice the power!

Step 4

TROUBLE TENSIONING

When you begin rigging tricklines with double the tension, the ratchet may start creating nicks in your webbing. This is caused by the slackline feeding unevenly into the ratchet, which can be difficult to correct when you're working at high tensions. For high-tension tricklines you will need to work with a teammate to maintain and correct the angle of feed.

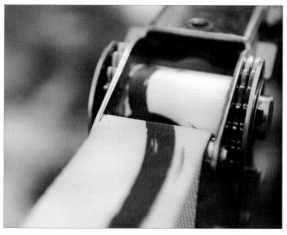

This ratchet is okay for now, but the webbing is feeding in too far to the left; correct your system at this point before the webbing begins to crush against the side of the ratchet and nick.

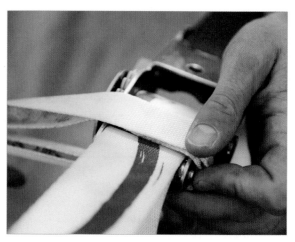

Use the excess webbing coming out the other end of the ratchet to pull the device in the opposite direction.

Andy had me pull the ratchet hard to the left as he cranked to re-center the webbing on the bolt.

After a few cranks with a partner pulling the ratchet, the webbing will re-center and you can continue tensioning as normal.

Scott Rogers performing the Warrior pose in Moab, Utah

Slackline Yoga:
Meet the YogaSlackers

Slackline yoga (or *slackasana*) has been described as "distilling the art of yogic concentration." An *asana* is simply a yoga position, and *slackasana* is the practice of yoga poses on the slackline. *Vinyasa* refers to linking sequences of these postures with focused breathing; *creating a vinyasa flow* on the slackline is what yoga slacklining is all about. A group known as YogaSlackers are leading the yoga slacklining movement. They describe the practice as one that "has many layers, simultaneously developing focus, dynamic balance, power, breath, core-integration, flexibility, and confidence. Utilizing standing postures, sitting postures, arm balances, kneeling postures, inversions, and unique vinyasa, a skilled slackline yogi is able to create a flowing yoga practice without ever falling from the line." The members of YogaSlackers have taught over 20,000 people how to embrace this arm of slacklining, and even developed a special line—the eLine by Trango—made of 1-inch webbing and rigged with a modified Ellington tensioning system to create the perfect medium for practitioners to create yoga flows on the slackline.

Just walking a slackline takes more focus than most people realize; attempting yoga positions on the line will hone your focus and balance skills to a fine point. Slackline yoga is the logical next step for slackers who have already mastered walking and balancing on the line. Start by trying a Warrior pose on the line, then move into the Buddha pose or Tree pose. Slackline yoga is achievable for almost anyone with patience and perseverance. Once you have begun to grasp the basic poses, difficulty can be increased by making the line longer or setting it at a lower tension.

Cassie Frantz
in Warrior pose

The Buddha pose is a classic static trick pulled from slackline yoga. Get low to the line, and use your hand as an aid to slide onto the outside edges of your feet. Remove both hands from the line to complete the pose.

Sam Salwei and Jason Magness founded YogaSlackers, an organization built around creating and teaching a yoga practice that can be done on the slackline. These slackasana pioneers took a moment to talk to me about what this arm of slacklining is all about and how to get started rigging and walking your own yoga slackline.

Q: How did YogaSlackers begin? What's it all about?

A: Team YogaSlackers has grown from the two of us, experimentally crossing disciplines that we love, to an eclectic mix of extreme endurance athletes, master yogis, rugged adventurers, and talented slackliners, who all share a passion for environmental education and awareness.

We first attempted slacklining during climbing trips at places like Patagonia base camp and Camp 4 in Yosemite. We struggled tremendously and had very little success. As experienced, semi-professional climbers it was difficult to be so challenged by slacklining and lack a clear idea of how to improve. We reapproached slacklining a few years later after discovering yoga. We were able to employ principles we had learned through yoga to slacklining—essentially treating it as a yoga practice.

This significant change in our mindset made learning more effective, fun, and safe. The slackline is an incredible tool for self-assessment and introspection. It's pretty profound to realize that *you* are the only thing that is actually causing the line to move and wiggle and wobble. Once you take ownership of that, you can really move forward.

Taking our yoga practice to the line led to the creation of YogaSlackers. We've now traveled all over the world teaching the practice we developed for the line. We've appeared in publications like *Climbing, Yoga Journal,* the *Wall Street Journal,* and *Outside.* We just completed our second teacher training and are continuing to expand to meet the growing demand. Our teachers hold classes, workshops, and retreats all over the country.

As for our slacklining preferences, we think it is important to play and practice on slacklines with a wide variety of lengths, materials, tensions, and even widths. Walking countless miles on lines of all sorts and teaching nearly 20,000 people the art of yoga slacklining led us to develop the eLine, which we designed based on our preferences for ease of setup, versatility, safety, and most important, feel.

Q: How do you rig a great yoga slackline (e.g., materials/brands if it makes a difference, tensioning system/preferred tension, length, anchors, ideal location)?

A: Yogaslacking is all about keeping it simple. We suggest using tubular polyester line with 11 percent stretch at 10 percent MBS (maximum breaking strength). This allows you to keep your tension system simple and lightweight. Yoga on the line will take you through many poses, changes in levels, and transitions. You will find yourself falling off the line many times as you practice, so another benefit of the Trango eLine is that it has very low "slap back." When we started teaching slackline yoga in 2005, we were using nylon lines with 22 to 30 percent stretch at 10 percent MBS. Our students would get so many bruises from being slapped by the line that we starting telling them to think of them as "slackline kisses" or "slackline hickeys."

Tension is a really important consideration when setting up your slackline for yoga. You want to find a tension more toward the slack side of the spectrum than the rigid side. With yogaslacking, or slackasana, it is very important to find a tension that helps you find a reflection of your energy rather than an amplification. You want to find a comfortable side-to-side swing, rather than tensioning the line so that it returns to center too quickly. Doing yoga on the line requires you to use your breath to release energy from the line, breathing the instability out of the line. Remember, the movement is coming from somewhere, and that somewhere is usually you! Doing yoga on the slackline helps you strengthen the stabilization muscles around your joints, which helps you control the movement. Strengthening these muscles and improving balance also helps prevent common injuries.

About 25 to 45 feet is a great length for a slackline. This allows you to complete a 15- to 20-minute vinyasa flow without coming off the line. Setting up in a park using trees for anchors is generally the preferred location.

Q: Do you have a proudest slackline achievement?

Sam: Creating YogaSlackers has been the most rewarding experience of my life. And deciding to dedicate my life to developing this organization was definitely a defining moment for me. We have grown from partners to a small amorphous group focused on extreme living with awareness.

I'm also proud of the fact that I've been able to refine my teaching and can now effectively share slacklining with almost anyone in less than 20 minutes.

Jason: Besides creating YogaSlackers, my proudest moment was watching my wife (and fellow YogaSlacker), whom I taught to slackline, walk her first 300-foot line on her first attempt . . . when it took me a long session to get across.

Another one was slacklining across the ocean (normally a Tyrolean) to climb the infamous Old Man of Stoer sea stack in Scotland.

Q: How would you describe your personal slackline philosophy/motivation?

Sam: What I seek most in slacklining is stillness. I spend about 270 days a year traveling. I am constantly on the move, and my mind is incessantly analyzing the world around me, trying to identify and solve problems. I only sleep when my body or mind are too exhausted to continue working. Life is constantly moving at a fast pace, and I'm able to empty my mind and find rest while doing yoga on the line.

Q: If someone wants to become a great yoga slackliner, what are three things they can do to get started on that path?

A: First, they can take a class with a YogaSlacker. YogaSlackers have developed a very clear way to share six fundamental modalities (sit, stand, arm balance, inversion, backbends, and kneeling). They have taught nearly 20,000 people to slackline since 2005. Classes are affordable with prices ranging from donation-based to around $40 for an intro class. YogaSlackers has fifty-nine certified teachers scattered across the United States, and many travel. You can find a class at www.YogaSlackers.com.

Second, they should acquire a slackline and practice. Building a community can aid the learning process, and we encourage groups of students that come to our workshops to get together frequently to practice.

Third, approach the line without expectations. Try not to focus on the number of steps or the amount of time you are able to stay on the line. Basically, you want to mix the intelligence of being an adult with the playfulness of being a child.

Q: What is the most important lesson you've learned as a rigger? And as a slackliner?

A: As a slacker: Sharing your passion creates the deepest level of satisfaction!

As a rigger: Attention to detail. As we started to explore the world of longlines, we learned that it is very important to pay close attention to MBS ratings, stay clear of rigging when possible, and back everything up! I have seen two lines over 300 feet long explode during tensioning. I even had a chain hoist yanked out of my hands when an anchor failed.

We slackline to prevent injury, not to create it by taking risks to impress others. We encourage you to develop your own practice that will be fun and allow you to find stillness in this busy world. Please practice responsibly.

CHAPTER THREE

Longlining

Intro to Rigging Longlines

The best way to learn how to rig safe slacklines is by starting out small and working your way up to longer, tighter, and higher lines. The consequences of rigging errors increase exponentially as you begin to rig lines with more tension and height. Start by rigging small lines so that you can gain some experience and learn from your mistakes in a safe environment.

One of the most dangerous misconceptions about slackline rigging is that it's the same as climbing rigging. Some principles regarding anchors are similar, but the rules are different in the slackline game. The forces you'll be dealing with are greater than the forces climbers learn to prepare for. No amount of technical knowledge can replace the lessons you'll learn through simple experience. Get lots of experience rigging lowlines before you move on to higher-consequence rigging on longlines and highlines.

Sketchy Rigging

What follows this section are a lot of numbers that describe three things:

- The force generated by your slackline.

- The relative strengths of slackline gear.

- How much of a margin you should leave between the two.

The first two values are known and can be measured objectively. The third value is left up to you. Slacklines are rigged all the time with gear barely strong enough to hold up to the forces exerted by the system; these lines are sketchy. Rigging a sketchy line can be exciting, and I encourage everyone to experiment with gear and techniques, *but in a safe environment.* Go ahead and push the limits if you want, as long as you remember that riggers have a responsibility to every single person that steps on their slackline. If your line is sketchy, let others know before they help you rig or walk. You alone are responsible for any accidents or gear failures that occur as a result of your own sketchy rigging.

Andy Lewis training on a long and heavy longline

Preparing to rig a longline

Understanding Slackline Forces

The most common mistake made by novice slack-line riggers is underestimating the amount of force their line will transfer to each anchor. It can be tempting to anchor your slackline to objects such as small trees, railings, or fence posts. However, these structures are not designed to withstand heavy loads; they can and have bent, broken, and ripped from the ground when used as slackline anchors.

Our intuition tells us that each anchor needs to be just strong enough to hold our own weight, plus the tension of the line. That's why it is so shocking when slacklines do things like rip off the tow-hitch of a truck (I've seen it happen) or break carabiners in an anchor.

It seems reasonable that each anchor should hold a portion of the slackliner's weight, just as your arms share the work of lifting a heavy object. However, the geometry involved in linking two anchors together with a slackline actually multiplies the load, causing each anchor to hold many times the normal weight of the person walking.

Longline anchors like this one bear a considerable amount of force.

The V-Angle

Consider this V-angle chart designed for rock climbing anchors. Climbers often equalize their anchors with a cordalette, distributing the downward force more or less equally between two points. The angle formed by the two arms of the cordalette is called a V-angle; at 20 degrees the weight is distributed evenly between both points. At 120 degrees the force on each anchor doubles. This is called load multiplication, and it's an exponential factor, skyrocketing as the angle approaches 180 degrees.

You can think of your slackline as a two-point anchor system with a V-angle approaching 180 degrees. This V-angle depends on the slackliner's weight, the length of the line, and the amount of sag. Sag is the amount of slack in the line, or how much the line moves vertically when weighted in the center. The tighter the slackline, the closer the V-angle comes to 180 degrees, creating extreme forces at each anchor. With more sag, the V-angle is smaller and safer.

Climbers consider V-angles greater than 120 degrees to be extremely dangerous. A broken sling or carabiner can be catastrophic for a climber, who is likely perched very high up the side of a cliff.

Slacklines almost always have V-angles between 120 and 180 degrees. Because force multiplication increases exponentially in that range, it's extremely difficult to predict exactly how much force any given slackline will generate. Slacklines can theoretically generate anywhere from 500 to 6,000 pounds of force (lbf) or more on each anchor.

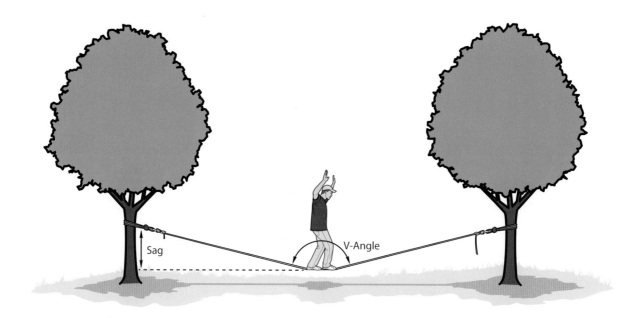

Sag is the vertical distance between the center of the slackline and the anchor slings when the line is being walked. The V-angle decreases as sag increases. Rig your lines with more sag to protect your equipment and anchors.

As a rule, slacklines put more force on the anchors as they increase in length and/or tension. Shorter slacklines and those with more sag will clock in closer to the lower end of the scale. If your slackline is less than 150 feet, it's very unlikely to exert more than 2,500 lbf. Extremely long lines and highlines have been measured at much higher values. The biggest number I've ever recorded on any slackline occurred on the (at the time) world record highline. It was 400 feet long and reached 6,000 lbf on a big fall.

Safe Enough

Deciding what's safe enough comes down to how much force you're generating and what happens if anything breaks. A broken sling on a lowline is no big deal, but the same situation on a highline could prove fatal. For practical purposes we can divide slacklines into two categories: high-consequence and low-consequence lines.

Low-consequence lines are shorter than 150 feet and low to the ground. Estimate 10kN force on each anchor.

High-consequence lines are longer than 150 feet or higher than a slackliner can fall without injury. Estimate 24kN force on each anchor.

Most lowlines are low-consequence lines. You can get away with making lots of mistakes and using weaker gear on low-consequence lines for two reasons: (1) You're unlikely to generate enough force to actually break anything; and (2) If something did break, there is no risk of serious injury.

Rigging high-consequence lines requires slackers to be much more cautious. The gear will be subject to greater forces, and/or the consequences of a broken slackline are much greater.

Once you've determined whether your line is low or high consequence, you can begin evaluating the relative strengths of your gear.

Webbing

Webbing is the material at the heart of the modern slackline movement. Dupont Chemical Company developed nylon for use in pantyhose, and only later during World War II saw its utility as a strong and light rope. The era following World War II saw a boom in climbing, especially in Yosemite Valley. Cheap army surplus carabiners and ropes were available in abundance, leading to new first ascents in rock climbing and the development of the first ever slackline made from carabiners and webbing by Jeff Ellington.

In essence a slackline is nothing more than a piece of webbing. All the other gear you will learn how to use in this guide functions only to anchor and tighten the webbing. Today there are a multitude of webbings available for slackliners, and different styles of walking and lengths of line are suited to different webbings. A piece of nylon webbing is perfect for a yoga slackline, but try rigging a longline with the same material and you may

Many different types of webbing are readily available for slacklining.

Units of Measurement

The tension of a slackline is always measured in pounds-force (lbf), where one lbf is equal to the amount of force generated by earth's gravity on a one-pound object. The international standard for measuring force is the newton. One newton is the amount of force required to accelerate a one-kilogram object at a rate of 1 meter per second squared. A kilonewton is a thousand newtons. Because newtons are based on motion and pound-force is based on earth's gravity, it is impossible to precisely convert one to the other. However, as long as you're rigging here on earth, it's safe to say that 1kN is approximately equal to 225 pounds. Slackline anchors generally hold anywhere from 2 to 24kN.

Abrasion

Regardless of how strong the webbing, rubbing against a foreign object will quickly snap a line of any strength. Webbing is particularly vulnerable to abrasion because of its thin, flat shape. Be sure to pad your webbing anywhere it comes into contact with anything besides the line locker.

find it much more difficult to send. Two slacklines of the same length rigged with different webbings will perform much differently, exhibiting different amounts of sway and stretch.

Slackliners typically find themselves gravitating to a "favorite" type of webbing, and there is no "best" webbing for a particular application. Slacklining styles are as variable as the personalities of the slackliners themselves. Fortunately, today webbing comes in a diverse array of colors, shapes, and materials to accommodate the diverse bunch of people that have taken up slacklining.

There are four main factors to consider when buying a piece of webbing: strength, weight, width, and percent stretch. This chapter is about how these factors affect longline rigging and walking, and to what degree each is displayed in different webbing materials and weaves.

Strength

Small slacklines very rarely generate enough force to break a piece of webbing, but longlines require much more tension (as much as 4,500 lbf). When a piece of webbing breaks under tension, pulleys and line lockers can launch into the air, injuring the people tensioning or sending the slackliner plummeting to the ground.

The important rating to look for when evaluating strength of slackline webbing is the breaking strength. Often listed as MBS (minimum breaking strength) as tested in a straight pull, this is sometimes listed beside the much higher value MBS as tested in a sewn loop, which is not relevant for

webbing rigged in a slackline. Be sure to determine how much force you are likely to generate with different line lengths and materials, and give yourself a safety margin of at least three times the maximum amount of force you are likely to put on your line. For instance, if I'm going to build a 100-foot line and generate 1,000 lbf, I need a line with an MBS in straight pull of at least 3,000 lbf.

Weight

Another factor that comes into play when choosing webbing for a line is its weight. Like width and flexibility, the weight of a piece of webbing affects the quality of your walk. Heavier webbing is generally more difficult to walk because it generates more momentum as it swings side to side, making it more difficult to control. You might choose a heavier line because it will be more durable or cheaper than high-tech webbings, but just be aware that it will be slightly more difficult to walk than the light stuff.

Width

The most popular webbings for any application are 1 inch wide. One-inch webbing can be found on everything from dog leashes to backpack straps. One-inch nylon webbing is one of the most common materials for building climbing anchors and is useful in a wide range of climbing applications. This was the webbing that the first slackliners in Yosemite used because they had it lying around to climb with, and classically this has been the width of choice for slackliners.

One-inch webbing is still generally considered to be the best width for highlines and longlines, but there's no reason to limit yourself to 1-inch line exclusively. Slacklines can be built from a variety of webbing widths, each of which gives the line unique properties.

In recent years the rise of tricklining has made wider webbings popular. Two-inch webbing has become the standard for tricklines because it gives slacklines an extra bouncy feel under high tension, making it possible to launch extremely high in the air. Two-inch has also been popular for beginner kits because, unlike 1-inch webbing, it can easily be rigged with a simple ratchet (almost exactly the same design as a cargo tie-down). One-inch webbing systems make a lot of sense for a climber who already has a pile of climbing anchors, carabiners, and rings that they know how to use. The 2-inch webbing and ratchet combo gives new slackers and non-climbers the opportunity to set up small lines easily and more cheaply.

The 2-inch webbing kits took a step away from climbing gear, lingo, and specialized knowledge, and brought a whole new set of people into the slacklining fold. Some of these new slackers used the bounciness of the 2-inch to take slacklining in an entirely new direction—tricklining.

Percent Stretch

Percent stretch refers to how much longer the line gets under tension, expressed as a percentage of the length of the total line. The percent stretch actually changes as tension increases (just as a rubber band will stretch farther if you pull it harder), until the pounds-force on the line exceed the breaking strength.

When I made my first big webbing purchase, to save some cash I made the mistake of buying 200 feet of mil spec, which is slightly cheaper than climbing-spec webbing. The problem was that when I tried to rig the full 200 feet, the line had so much stretch I couldn't pull enough tension on the line to support my weight walking across. It stretched to the grass and bottomed out every time. I actually had to break down and buy a longer pulley rope so I could extend my pulleys a greater distance (the linegrip hadn't been invented yet). It seemed like I spent hours trying to set up that line and pull out all the slack. Finally I rigged and walked the thing, but in the end I didn't save any money, and pulling out so much webbing was tedious and tiring. I never bought mil spec for a longline again. Lower-stretch webbings are far easier to rig because you don't need to pull out so much slack. Some of the new webbings barely need to be tensioned at all.

Percent stretch is one of the most important factors to consider when choosing webbing because it affects so many slacklining factors, from rigging to walking to safety. It's helpful to know the approximate percent stretch of the webbing you're rigging when setting up your pulleys. If you know the distance between your anchors, and you know that your percent stretch is X, you can calculate X percent of the distance, and that value is how long your pulleys need to be.

More than any other webbing trait, stretch affects the quality of your walk. High-stretch lines are ideal for tricklining; very dynamic webbings make high-amplitude jumps and powerful surfs possible. Low-stretch lines make great longlines because of their stability and ease of rigging. They also make great highlines and shorter slacklines when rigged under very low tension. It is much easier to walk low-stretch webbing under low tension than high-stretch webbing under the same tension. If you want to walk a rodeo line (no tension), low-stretch webbing is for you.

Stretch plays a role in strength as well. A high-stretch line will absorb much of the force of a dynamic fall, slowing it down as the line stretches. As percent stretch creeps lower, MBS creeps higher because static materials have a limited ability to absorb the shock load of a falling slackliner.

Types of Webbing

NYLON

The most basic way to classify webbing is by the material of the fibers it is woven with. I already mentioned mil-spec and climbing-spec webbings. Both of these slackline webbings are made of nylon woven into a flattened, tubular shape. The main difference between the two types is that one is rated to climbing specifications and the other to military standards. The climbing-spec webbing has a higher thread count and finer weave, which makes it significantly softer. Climb spec has a lower percent stretch and higher maximum breaking strength than mil spec. Climb-spec slacklines generally feel better to walk and are easier to rig.

Tubular nylon slackline (climb spec) is often threaded with ⁹⁄₁₆-inch webbing through the middle. This is called a threaded line and was originally intended to increase highline safety by creating a second line within the first to act as a backup in case the outer webbing snapped. However, in tests both pieces were shown to break simultaneously, so the threaded line is not truly redundant. Still, it feels good to walk on and is soft and stronger (around two times stronger) than an unthreaded line, so the threaded nylon lines remain popular with slackliners of all styles.

Type-18 is nylon woven in a flat shape, using the same material but with a different weave. The flat shape creates slightly different properties of sway and hand or feel of the webbing.

Tubular nylon webbing is the classic choice for tricklines and slacklines under 150 feet. This material stretches about 15 percent at average slackline tension, making it the most dynamic material to slackline on. The stretch of nylon slacklines is what attracted the first slackers. The dynamic material allows athletes to execute big movements like flips and surfs. Tubular nylon is still popular because it feels great underneath the feet. Highline catches on threaded tubular are as soft as it gets, making this the webbing of choice for many beginning highliners. It costs less than a dollar per foot, which makes it affordable, and nylon doesn't deteriorate with age, so your line should last a long time.

The elastic quality that makes nylon so great, however, is also its downfall when it comes to rigging very long lines. Rigging nylon over 150 feet is a chore. At 15 percent stretch, a 200-foot nylon line needs around 30 feet pulled out to reach walkable tension! If that doesn't sound like a lot, remember that this means you'll end up pulling, with pulleys, the end of your rope 150 feet.

POLYESTER

Polyester, aka Dacron or Terylene, was developed in the 1940s. Usually woven in a flat shape, the critical difference for slackliners is the reduction of elasticity that polyester webbings offer. Polyester fibers stretch only 3.5 to 5 percent at low tension. This low elongation means two things for slackliners: a more stable longline, and less pulling to reach walkable tension. Nylon webbing will always be a staple of slacklining equipment, but polyester is quickly becoming more popular as slackliners find they can walk longer distances and rig their lines more easily with polyester webbing like Gibbon's Proline and Flowline, as well as Mantra and White Magic.

VECTRAN

Some of the newest webbings are made of Vectran fibers. Vectran has long been the holy grail of longlines. Its low weight and low stretch combined with durability and extremely high strength make it possible to rig walkable lines longer than ever before. The longer a line is, the more force needs to be applied to the webbing to reach walkable tension. At some point the force needed exceeds the breaking strength of certain webbing types. With Vectran it's possible to rig lines over 1,000 feet long without approaching the breaking strength of the webbing. The downside with Vectran and other high-tech webbings is the cost. Vectran is many times more expensive per foot than polyester or nylon webbings, and since its utility is only realized in very long lines, Vectran can be a prohibitively expensive investment.

Longline Hardware

Climbing gear has an undeserved reputation for being extremely strong. For climbing purposes it's fine, but slackline rigging is an entirely different game, with a different set of rules. Slackliners cannot place their trust in manufacturers the way climbers can, using gear "rated for climbing" without a second thought. There is almost no gear "rated for slacklining," but most gear has its technical specs engraved or stamped somewhere on it, and once you know what type of line you want, it's relatively easy to find the type of gear you need.

The important rating to look for when evaluating the strength of slackline gear is the *minimum breaking strength*. It's a rigger's responsibility to know the MBS of every single piece of gear in their system. Always use gear with an MBS that is more than the amount of force you plan on generating.

This is called rigging with a safety factor. Each

A leverhoist is a common piece of equipment used by longliners.

rigger should decide what safety factor they feel comfortable with. For the purposes of this guide, a low-consequence slackline is safe enough when it can hold twice as much as the greatest force a slackliner could possibly put on it—a safety factor of 2. For high-consequence lines the safety factor should be 3 or more.

To calculate the safety factor for any article of gear, divide the listed MBS by the predicted value for force.

For instance, an aluminum climbing carabiner is rated to 25kN. For a low-consequence line, estimate 10kN for force. The rating of 25 divided by a force of 10 gives us a safety factor of 2.5. The gear is two and a half times stronger than the maximum force that will be exerted on it.

If you're rigging a longline with the same carabiner, your safety factor is 25kN/24kN, only a little more than 1. That means the gear is just barely strong enough to hold the line's tension without breaking. Ultimately how comfortable you feel with that number is up to you.

For slacklines under 150 feet, the greatest probable force is 10kN, so all the anchor components should have an MBS of at least 20kN—which means that climbing gear is safe to use on these lines.

Longlines and highlines that are likely to generate more than 10kN must be rigged with specialized rigging equipment or steel climbing carabiners. A 3:1 safety ratio for these types of lines means all anchor materials should have an MBS of more than 30kN. For a more conservative estimate, use 24kN (my highest ever recorded value for slackline tension), which gives you a baseline rating of 72kN MBS for slacklining gear.

Carabiners

Carabiners, called biners (BEAN-ers) for short, are oval-shaped links made of aluminum or steel with spring-loaded gates, used in climbing to link the rope and climbers into the anchors. Carabiners are available in great variety; even the smallest gear shop will carry at least a dozen different kinds, all designed with a different application in mind. Unfortunately, none of them are designed specifically for slacklining, so what follows are the criteria for a good slacklining biner, in order of importance.

STRENGTH RATING

The abbreviation kN stands for kilonewton, and it appears on almost every carabiner. The numbers listed here are the MBS of the carabiner when loaded in different directions, as indicated by the direction the arrows point. Carabiners are strongest when loaded along their long axis; the one in the photo has an MBS of 26kN when loaded correctly along the long axis. It's only half as strong (12kN) when loaded in the opposite direction, or crossloaded. The third symbol shows a carabiner with an open gate; this biner has an MBS of only 7kN when its gate is opened. The last symbol indicates how much force is required to break the gate open from the outside after it's locked, which is 6kN for the orange Pirate carabiner shown on facing page bottom left.

The CE marking is a certification for imports to European countries. The number that follows identifies the "notified body," or the third party, that the CE authorized to say that this carabiner is safe. Short for Conformité Européenne, the CE marking can be found printed on everything from toasters to hospital beds. UIAA is another acronym you'll see printed on biners and ropes. It stands for the International Climbing and Mountaineering Federation. Unfortunately, for slackline rigging the CE and UIAA markings are pretty useless. The tests this carabiner went through were not designed to simulate slackline-type loading. It's your responsibility as a rigger to know the MBS of your gear and judge its safety for yourself.

Carabiners come in an array of shapes, styles, and materials.

Every biner has a jumble of letters, numbers, and little drawings on its spine. It's important to know what at least some of them mean.

The strengths are often listed with slightly different symbols, which may also be in a different order.

This DMM auto-locking belay carabiner is marked on the outside edge of the spine. The long sequence of numbers below is an individual ID number; these can help the manufacturer determine the cause of failure in case of an accident.

Loading a Carabiner

Orient your biners so that they are being pulled in the strongest configuration: along their long axis. Cross-loaded and tri-loaded biners may break under slackline tension. Make sure all biners are oriented correctly before you pull tension on your line.

Carabiners can lose more than half their strength when used incorrectly.

STEEL OR ALUMINUM?

There have been cases of aluminum carabiners breaking when used for slackline rigging. Steel carabiners are generally around twice as strong as aluminum carabiners. In addition steel carabiners retain their strength for much longer. Aluminum can develop microscopic cracks from repeated loading and unloading. This doesn't pose a problem in climbing, where the biner is only weighted if the climber falls, but when the biner must repeatedly hold large static loads, as in slacklining, aluminum can weaken enough to snap under tension.

Steel carabiners are regularly used to hold large loads in rescue applications, are much less vulnerable to metal fatigue, and have never been reported to break when used in slackline anchors. Steel biners are a must for longline and highline rigging. Aluminum doesn't provide enough of a cushion between the MBS (25kN) and predicted loading (24kN) to create an adequate safety factor for high-consequence slacklines.

LOCKING MECHANISMS

A locking gate ensures that the gate on a biner closes fully and stays closed. Unless used in a primitive system, all slackline carabiners should have locking gates. A carabiner can lose as much as three-quarters of its strength when the gate is open. The forces on a slackline anchor may be enough to destroy an aluminum carabiner with an open gate. Use locking carabiners, and always check nonlocking carabiners to ensure that their gates are fully closed before and after tensioning your slackline.

A locking carabiner doesn't do much good if you forget to lock it. Auto-locking biners have spring-loaded locking mechanisms that lock the gate automatically.

Carabiners are more flexible than you think. Try to open a loaded carabiner after pulling tension on your slackline. Can't do it? That's because your slackline stretched the carabiner lengthwise, effectively "locking" it closed. The gate is a load-bearing part of a carabiner; if it's not fully shut, slackline tension can stretch a carabiner far enough to break!

The markings on a steel biner may look slightly different than those on an aluminum biner. This steel D has an MBS of 72kN. From there you can infer that the MBS in a cross-loaded or tri-loaded configuration is likely as much as 18kN. Steel biners leave a lot more room for user error than aluminum biners; a steel biner will hold your slackline in configurations where aluminum would snap.

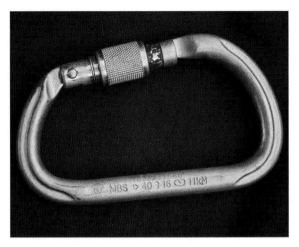

The red paint showing above the lock on this carabiner indicates that the biner is in the "unlocked" position.

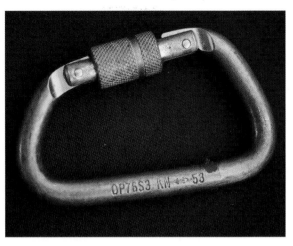

This carabiner is unlocked too, but has no warning symbol. Always give your locking biners a physical test, pushing on the outside of the gate, to ensure they are locked.

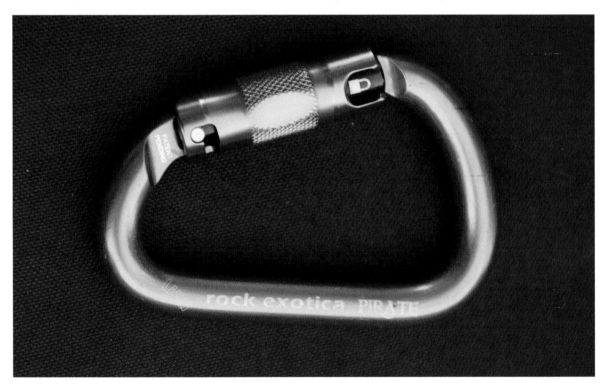

An auto-locking aluminum biner—the closed lock symbol here indicates that this biner is in the locked position.

SHAPE

The best carabiner shape for static rigging is a symmetric oval. Most carabiners are asymmetric. Symmetrical shapes won't shift under load, while D or pear-shaped biners will shift after tensioning, so that the load pulls along the spine of the biner.

All carabiner shapes are useful for different applications in slackline rigging. Consider what you intend to link together with each carabiner. Large, rounded carabiners work well for anchoring bulky spansets, but tiblocs and some small pulleys will require a thinner carabiner. Most slackline systems will incorporate at least two different carabiner shapes.

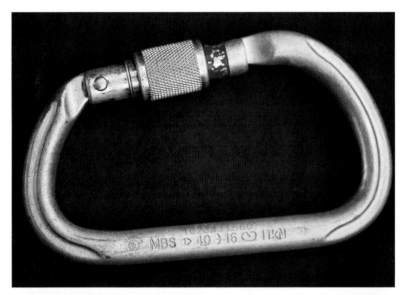

A slightly asymmetric oval steel biner

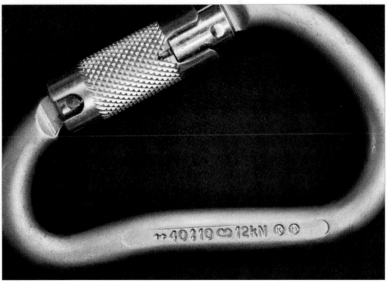

A pear-shaped steel biner

Shackles

A shackle is a U-shaped connecting link secured with a bolt; it's used in all sorts of rigging. A carabiner is actually a variety of shackle. When I first saw longlines rigged with shackles, I was skeptical. My climbing background had made me biased against hardware store gear, and shackles looked cheaply made next to the shiny, anodized climbing biners I had learned to trust. But despite their appearance steel shackles are actually designed for heavier loads than carabiners.

Steel shackles are a good alternative to steel carabiners for many rigging applications. They retain more of their strength in cross- or tri-loaded configurations and are a better shape for building line lockers (see page 111). Shackles can be used as rigging plates to link pulleys together, and smaller shackles sometimes fit places where a carabiner will not.

SHACKLE STRENGTH

Shackles are not climbing gear. They are industrial rigging gear, and all industrial rigging gear is marked with a working load limit instead of minimum breaking strength.

Riggers should always know the MBS of *all* the gear in their slackline. It's very important to know the source of your shackles so you can visit the manufacturer's website to see what safety factor was used to calculate the working load limit. Buy shackles from reputable North American manufacturers such as Crosby, VanBeest, or Peer-Lift. There have been incidents of imported shackles reportedly failing at loads significantly less than their WLL. If you don't know where the shackle came from, think twice before using it.

Quick Links

Don't be fooled by the name: Quick links are just about the slowest way to connect anchor components. However, quick links are extremely strong for their weight. They make great bolt attachments for slackline bolts; a rope can run through a quick link with very little friction; and once they're closed they stay that way. You can even wrench quick links tight for a semipermanent closure.

It's a good idea to keep one or two quick links with your slackline kit or on your harness. They make a great emergency substitute for carabiners

An assortment of shackles are useful in slackline rigging.

You can take the pin out of a large shackle and thread two smaller shackles through the bolt holes to make a rigging plate for pulleys.

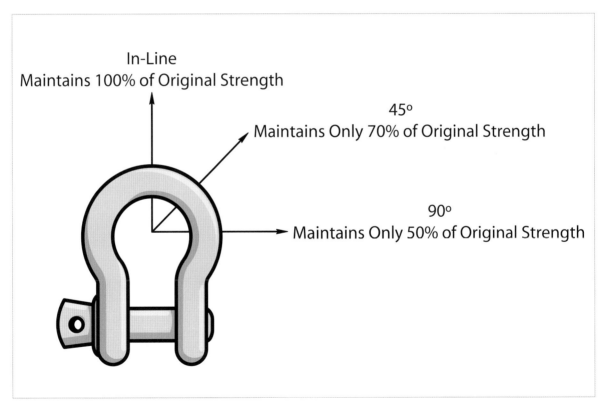

In-Line
Maintains 100% of Original Strength

45°
Maintains Only 70% of Original Strength

90°
Maintains Only 50% of Original Strength

Shackles are stronger than carabiners when cross-loaded or tri-loaded.

Working Load Limit (WLL)

$\mathbb{A}$ ll industrial rigging gear (including shackles and spansets) is marked with a *working load limit* instead of a *minimum breaking strength.* What this means is that a safety factor is already calculated into the strength rating. The working load limit is a fraction of the MBS. The trouble with this system, however, is that neither climbing gear nor industrial gear states whether the value printed is WLL or MBS. In addition the safety factor used to calculate WLL could be anywhere from 15 to 3. This makes comparing relative strengths of gear very difficult. Remember that all climbing gear is marked with its MBS, and any values engraved on rigging gear are WLL calculated with a safety factor of at least 2.

Figuring out the strength rating of this shackle will take a little math. It's a ⅝-inch shackle with a WLL of 3.25 tons. Peer-Lift shackles have a 6:1 safety ratio, so the MBS of this shackle is over 19.5 tons. That's more than 150kN, six times the strength of an aluminum biner!

Quick links are like chain links but have a screw-action gate.

and shackles. The strength of quick links varies, and the MBS is not typically engraved on the spine. Buy your quick links from a reputable manufacturer and know the MBS before you make them part of your anchors.

Line Lockers

Longlines require stronger line lockers than beginner slacklines because the webbing in a longline is subjected to much higher tensions.

SLEEVED LINE LOCKERS

To add durability to the locker for high-tension lines, highlines, or semipermanent lines, use a piece of tubular webbing as a sleeve for your line locker, and incorporate two rings instead of one. A shackle works better than a carabiner to keep the line flat, but a very large locking steel carabiner can be substituted for the shackle. The sleeve adds bulk to the webbing as it goes through the locker, making the whole hitch bigger and slightly more difficult to tie. Because these lockers are for high-tension lines, when building a sleeved line locker it's important to be extremely careful that all the layers of webbing lie flat.

Gear

- 3 or more feet of 2-inch tubular webbing
- Two aluminum or steel 2-inch rings
- One shackle or steel carabiner

Sleeving the Line

New 2-inch webbing will have a deep crease on both sides and may be slightly melted together at the ends. If this is the case, cut a little webbing off each end so you can open the tubular webbing. To prevent fraying on the sleeve, re-melt the edges of the tube with a lighter, holding it open so it doesn't melt together again as it cools.

Melting a webbing sleeve with a lighter to prevent fraying

1. Open the webbing and fold it in half, flattening the creases on each edge to make it easier to slide your slackline through.
2. From a standing position, hold the sleeve out away from your body and lower the slackline through the sleeve slowly. This won't work if you're sitting; you need the sleeve to be free hanging so gravity can help pull the webbing down and through.
3. Pull the slackline through when it reaches the end. Leave enough tail to tie a backup knot later.

Step 2

Step 3

Dots Up

I've rigged my slackline in these photos with dots "up," meaning the dots will point toward the sky when rigged, on both the line and sleeve. Rigging dots-up makes it easier to avoid twists in the line, because it's always easy to see which side is supposed to be up. Most webbing has dots or some kind of pattern on one side; think twice before buying webbing with no markings or markings on both sides, because it makes keeping your webbing flat very difficult, especially on longer lines.

4. A crease inside the sleeve could nick the line under high tension. Run the sleeve through your hands a few times, checking for flips.
5. Once the webbing is threaded, fold a bight in the middle of the sleeve and slide two rings onto the bight.

6. Make a *big* circle with your webbing, folding the bight over the rings and back toward the tail side.

Step 6

7. Pull the head of the bight through the rings.

Step 5

Step 7

8. Spread the bight wide to make one huge circle of webbing.

9. Clip a carabiner through the bight.

Step 8

Step 9

10. Pull the bottom tail first, to set the line locker without creasing.

11. Pull the top line last to finish the line locker.

Step 10

Step 11

The line locker should look like this after step

ADJUSTABLE LINE LOCKERS

The placement of the line locker can get tricky when rigging longlines, soft-pointing slacklines, or highlines near an edge. Adjustable line lockers make it easy to slide webbing through the locker in one direction. You can make your line shorter as long as there is very little tension on the webbing. It's even possible to put a small amount of tension on the line just by pulling it through an adjustable line locker. Adjustable line lockers are designed to hold webbing flat through the whole system, so there's no need for a sleeve.

You'll need any type of adjustable line locker, such as an Alpine Weblock, Gibbon Weblock, or MONSTER Lock.

1. Slide the moving bolt up and partially out of the line locker.

Step 1

2. Bring a bight of the webbing up through the concave side of the line locker, between the two permanent bolts.

Step 2

3. Hold the head of the bight open and push the moving bolt back into place, through the head of the bight.

Step 3

4. Pull the webbing tight and clip the weblock to the master point of the anchor with a locking carabiner. The walking webbing should be on top.

Step 4

5. Pull as much slack as possible through the weblock before tensioning by pulling the tail of the slackline through (the bottom piece of webbing exiting the weblock).

Step 5

Step 6

6. Back up the weblock by tying the tail off to the master point of the slackline anchor.

Tensioning Longlines

Longlines require much more tension than the slacklines described so far in this guide. To tension a longline, you will need a slackline pulley kit, a set of pulleys and a rigging plate, or a chain hoist system. While the chain hoist is a relatively new addition to slackline rigging, pulleys have been around as long as slacklining has. The Ellington is basically a simplified pulley system using carabiners instead of the bulkier, more expensive pulleys used for longlining and highlining. Generally pulleys fall outside the realm of backyard, or beginner, slacklining. They are absolutely essential for longlines, however, and they can also be used to get your 1-inch webbing tighter for tricklining. You can easily link pulleys to any 2-inch slackline kit by making a line locker with 2-inch rings and linking that to the end of the pulleys.

An efficient pulley system helps a lot for tensioning longlines.

Use a 2-inch ring to make a line locker for your trickline webbing. Link to the pulleys with a locking carabiner.

Building Custom Slackline Pulley Systems

Most slackline pulley systems are built with what is called a block and tackle. A block and tackle is rigged using two or more opposing pulleys with a rope threaded through them. One end of the rope is attached to a ring, or becket, on one block, and the other end is threaded through the pulleys and pulled to tighten the system. The arrangement of the ropes essentially divides the force between all of the ropes. This creates mechanical advantage, which is usually expressed as a ratio. A 4:1 pulley system would theoretically enable someone to lift a one hundred–pound load by applying only twenty-five pounds of force. The block and tackle has a 4:1 mechanical advantage and is one of the simplest and most efficient ways to tension a longline.

A 4:1 system built on a double block and tackle
HAYLEY ASHBURN

Combine two double pulleys to create a quadruple block and tackle system with an 8:1 mechanical advantage for super long lines.
HAYLEY ASHBURN

The mechanical advantage ratio is easy to determine just by looking at the pulleys. Count the number of ropes under tension in a pulley system to calculate the mechanical advantage (not counting the rope used for pulling). It is always that number to one.

MECHANICAL ADVANTAGE AND EFFICIENCY

The mechanical advantage is only a theoretical value because it assumes that no energy is lost to friction. There will always be some friction in your system, but it's possible to increase efficiency by selecting the correct pulleys. The turning piece inside a pulley is called the sheave. Know whether your pulleys are built with bearings or bushings for the sheave. Bushings are simply a metal cylinder that turns around the axis of the pulley; the entire circumference of the bushing rolls around the axis of the pulley, creating lots of friction. Ball bearings are much more efficient; their outer surface rolls along a series of small beads. The rope transfers force to the axis through the beads, reducing the surface area rubbing against the axis and minimizing friction. Ball bearings are available in two types: sealed and unsealed, which simply means that the layers of the sheave are either left open to the elements or protected. Sand and dirt can easily work their way into unsealed bearings, creating unwanted friction.

Once you know if your sheaves have bearings or bushings and whether or not they are sealed, consider the sheave diameter. Pulleys with a larger sheave will be more efficient; the farther away from the center of a wheel you are, the easier it will be to spin that wheel. Smaller pulleys have the advantage of being lightweight, but are generally less efficient because of their smaller sheave diameter.

BRAKES

In addition to a pulley system, you will need a brake to capture progress on the pulling rope. The brake holds tension on the pulley rope and slack-line even after all the pullers have let go. The brake

A Petzl Gri-Gri rigged as a brake

The end you pull should come out of the device on the side showing the hand.

is added to the pulley system on the opposite side of the point where the rope exits the last pulley. Belay devices are the most common pulley system brakes used by slackliners. The Petzl Gri-Gri and ID as well as the Trango Cinch are all belay devices that can be safely used as brakes on slackline pulley systems. The Gri-Gri and Cinch have less holding power than the ID, but are less expensive. Use the ID to rig lines over 300 feet long. For all these belay devices, feed the rope into the device with the tail, or pulling end, coming out of the part of the device with a hand symbol. The device will then brake in the direction of the climber symbol. If you're confused about which way to thread the rope into the device, simply try rigging it in either direction; you'll know you've got it right when you can pull rope through on the tail side. When you've reached the right tension, tie an overhand knot on a bight to back up the brake. Seat the knot as close to the brake as possible. This way, if your brake fails, the knot will keep the tail of the pulley rope from being pulled through.

PULLEY ROPES

You will need a rope of 100 feet or longer to build a slackline pulley system. Always use static rope to thread your pulleys, or you will spend energy stretching out the rope within the system. A static rope transfers your energy more efficiently. Besides length and stretch, consider the diameter of the rope you use. Very thin rope is difficult to pull without injuring your hands, but rope that is too thick may rub against the sides of the pulley, reducing efficiency. Most pulleys are marked for their ideal rope diameter, somewhere between 8 and 10 millimeters.

THREADING PULLEYS

1. Find a static rope that fits easily into your pulleys (too wide a rope will create friction on the housing) and tie one end to the becket on either block.

Step 1

HAYLEY ASHBURN

2. Next, thread your rope under and over the far pulley on the opposite block.

Step 2

HAYLEY ASHBURN

3. Bring the rope back to the other block and thread it over and under the far pulley.

Step 3

HAYLEY ASHBURN

5. Thread the rope over and under the last open pulley.

Step 5

HAYLEY ASHBURN

4. Bring the rope back across to the opposite block and thread under and over the near pulley.

Step 4

HAYLEY ASHBURN

6. Thread the brake as shown in the instructions for the device you are using.

Step 6

HAYLEY ASHBURN

ALIGNING THE BRAKE

One block of pulleys will link to the master point of your anchor and is called the fixed end; the other will link to the line locker on your slackline and is called the moving end. Unless you are using the SBI kit with the integrated brake, the brake has its own becket and requires its own anchor. The key to rigging an efficient brake is to align it as closely as possible with the pulleys. If the primary anchor is a tree, rig the brake to a second sling beneath the main anchor for the least gear–intensive method for rigging the brake.

The most efficient placement of the brake is achieved with a shackle or rigging plate. Clip one of these to the sling to create several master points where the pulley block and the brake can be rigged side by side.

A rigging plate with a Petzl ID brake

Using a shackle instead of an expensive rigging plate is the best way I've found to keep pulleys in line.

HAYLEY ASHBURN

Making a Multiplier

It's absolutely essential to multiply. A multiplier does just what it sounds like—it multiplies your mechanical advantage. Using a multiplier makes it around six times easier to pull the rope on a 4:1 system. It's definitely worth the $30 it'll cost you to buy the gear. You will need a tibloc or other prusik device, a small pulley, and a small, non-locking carabiner to build a multiplier.

1. Place your tibloc on the segment of rope going into the brake, with the skinny end of the tibloc pointing to the brake.
2. Open your small pulley, insert the tail of the rope into the pulley, and clip to the tibloc as shown.
3. Pull with all your might.

A tibloc multiplier

THE ECONOMY MULTIPLIER

Like most other systems in slackline rigging, there is more than one way to skin a cat when it comes to building a multiplier. Try replacing the tibloc with a prusik for less than half the cost. The prusik is a rope-gripping hitch tied with small-diameter cord or a piece of webbing. A prusik uses friction to lock the cord around the rope, so the harder you pull, the harder a prusik will grip. Any rope-grabbing device will slip under too much tension, and those with metal teeth like tiblocs and ascenders may damage the sheath. A prusik will slip at lower tensions, but it will never damage your rope when used as a multiplier.

To make a prusik cord, tie a piece of 7 or 8 millimeter cord into a continuous loop using a double fisherman's knot. Hold the loop by the knot and girth-hitch it loosely around the line so the knot hangs below the hitch and out of the way. Then wrap the knot several more times around the rope (the more times the cord goes around the rope, the stronger the hitch will be). Clip a carabiner through the hanging loop and attach a pulley for your multiplier. The prusik will grip when activated by the pulley, but should slide easily along the rope when pushed in either direction with a hand on the wrapped portion.

THE HOBO MULTIPLIER

If you find yourself at the slackline without any multiplier gear, you can use this last method for an emergency quick fix using nothing but a single carabiner. The hobo multiplier requires tying a knot in the pulley rope, which can be difficult to untie, so I usually try to find some extra people to help pull before resorting to this method. Tie a loop in the pulley rope where you would normally place the tibloc. An overhand on a bight works best. Then clip a carabiner through the loop and run the pulling end through the biner to rig a makeshift pulley. You'll lose a lot of efficiency to friction, but it's still miles better than a pulley system with no multiplier at all. A last note about the hobo multiplier: Make sure to untie your overhand before de-tensioning the line, or it will get hopelessly stuck in the pulley and ruin your day.

Soft-Pointing with the Linegrip and Chain Hoist

Often times a tensioning system is heavy and adds unwanted weight to a slackline. This weight makes it harder to walk, so you may wish to Soft-Point your slackline, or remove your tensioning system from the line before walking.

Start by building your main anchor; this will be the anchor that holds the slackline during your session. Attach the slackline webbing to an adjustable line locker on the master point. Pull out as much slack as possible by pulling webbing through the line locker.

Build a second anchor for the tensioning system, as close as possible to the main anchor. The second anchor can be rigged to a different tree, or just to a separate sling above or below the main anchor. Positioning the second anchor too far to the side, or radically above or below the main anchor, will pull the slackline out of line. This can cause the line to lose extra tension when transferring to the main anchor.

Apply the linegrip to the hand-tensioned slackline. My tensioning system hangs below the main anchor, so I'll position my linegrip with its anchor point below the webbing. If your tensioning anchor is above your main anchor, rest the linegrip on top of the line.

The linegrip is one of the greatest recent innovations in rigging technology.

Here, I've used a rigging plate to make two master points on my main anchor. This technique will keep the main line and tensioning systems as close together as possible, and eliminates the need to build two anchors.

Linegrip pulling tension on the webbing

Holding tension on the linegrip

Pull accumulating slack through the adjustable line locker to minimize clutter at the anchor.

Attach the tail of the webbing to the main anchor with a loose overhand on a bight to back up the line locker. Always leave some slack in the webbing here. A very small amount may slip through the line locker during normal use, making this backup very difficult to remove if tied too close to the locker.

After cranking some tension on the chain hoist, slack will build up in the main anchor system behind the linegrip. Pulling this slack out of the system is how a soft-pointed line stays tensioned.

When you've reached the desired tension, pull out as much slack as possible. Keep in mind that some tension will always be lost in the final stages of soft-pointing as a result of slack in the system. To adjust for this effect, tension the line slightly more than you normally would and try to minimize the amount of slack left in the webbing between the linegrip and line locker.

When you release the tensioning system, the force of the line will shift to the main anchor. At this point the linegrip will easily release, and the tensioning system can be removed.

DE-TENSIONING

To de-tension a soft-pointed slackline, reset the tensioning system to the secondary anchor and pull tension on the webbing using the linegrip. Let enough slack build up in the main anchor so that you can easily detach the slackline from the master point. Untie any backups from the master point; the linegrip should be the only thing holding the webbing. Release the tensioning system and de-rig as normal.

Highline Skills

In 1983 Scott Balcom, Chris Carpenter, and Chongo Tucker took the sport of slacklining a huge leap forward when they built the world's first highline in Pasadena, California, under a local bridge. Two years later Balcom broke Philippe Petit's record for highest line (formerly the Twin Towers at 1,368 feet) when he walked the famous Lost Arrow Spire Highline. Perched between a granite cliff and a delicate finger of stone some 2,890 feet above Yosemite Valley, this line has become the most famous and sought after in the world.

Balcolm's historic walk inspired a new generation to push the limits of slacklining. Americans had been admiring highwire walkers since Petit's famous walk of the Twin Towers, and now there was an easily accessible way to highwire on their own. Slacklining slowly gained popularity throughout the 1990s, then started to pick up speed at the beginning of the new millennium.

This new arm of slacklining, part pure recklessness and part serious focus, began to fascinate young people all over the United States, especially in California. Dean Potter, already one of Yosemite's best climbers, became a legend in modern slacklining with his many bold highline free solos, including the Lost Arrow Spire. Darrin Carter was the first to free solo the Lost Arrow Spire Highline, long before Potter. The Spire line is around 50 feet long; today, a mere thirty years later, the world record for the longest highline is 435 feet. Large groups of slackliners can be found gathered at the Spire in the summer months, and the increasing popularity of highlining has not only pushed those in the upper levels of the sport to greater heights, but it has also opened up the highlining community to slackliners of all ability levels and backgrounds. Many highliners today are not climbers, and they don't need to be. There are thousands of potential highlines in the world that can be rigged with little or no roped climbing. Some knowledge of basic climbing safety gear is *essential* to stay safe on a highline, and a great deal of knowledge is required to rig a safe highline, but walking your first highline is an achievable goal for *any* slackliner.

Walking your first highline will be one of the most exciting and demanding challenges you will ever encounter. You will need to familiarize yourself with safety gear and techniques for falling and mounting the line before you can even attempt your first highline walk. Struggling with the basic highline mounting and catching skills can be a roadblock for slackers who would otherwise send a line easily. More than anything else, highlining is a test of courage; doing some basic training will make you mentally as well as physically prepared for your first walk. What follows are a few basic skills that will make your first walk go a lot smoother.

I'm walking a line between the Dolomite Spire and the Lighthouse Tower in Utah.

Legendary highliner Faith Dickey only became a rock climber after walking her first highlines.

Training for Aspiring Highliners

Highline training is all about challenging yourself to walk the heaviest and longest lines possible. Highlines typically feel at least twice as long and heavy as they really are, even without the addition of fear. Because all proper highlines are rigged redundantly, you are walking on twice the webbing and thus twice the weight. This increased weight makes the line much harder. Increase length as well as weight on your slacklines to prepare for this effect. If you can easily walk a 100- or 150-foot slackline with an extra piece of webbing, or an added backup rope, you can consider yourself well prepared for a 50-foot or shorter highline.

Cassie Frantz practicing on a highline

If you can easily walk a line, challenge yourself by doing something harder like mounting in the middle or releasing some tension from the line. Or try mounting without touching the ground to simulate a highline. You need to really push your limits near the ground before you're ready to do it up high.

Cables and chains are the heaviest mediums that exist for slacklining. If you can find one, even a short cable or chain is great highlining practice, not to mention simply great fun on a radically new type of line.

Your core muscles will gain strength through high-weight-line training, which will prepare you for the physical aspects of highlining, but your main challenge will still be mental. Highlining is a battle between the body and the mind. Maintaining focus becomes extremely difficult when the mind is under stress. Longlining can help you cope by training your ability to stay focused for long periods of time. You will be walking more slowly than normal on a highline, so even a short distance can take what seems like forever to cross. Strive to walk longer lines to challenge your ability to maintain focus for long periods of time. Challenge yourself by rigging lines higher, longer, and heavier than you've ever walked before. The increased weight will make you stronger and, more importantly, better able to focus in any situation.

The Mock Highline

Build a mock highline by taping a second piece of webbing or rope underneath your slackline at home. You'll need electrical tape and a rope (any size and strength will do, generally the bigger the

This 200-foot training line has a second piece of webbing and a rope taped to the bottom to make it as heavy and difficult as possible.

better). After your slackline is tensioned, clip or tie each end of the rope to the master points of the anchors. Get the rope as tight as possible without using a tensioning system. For longlines you may need to pull the rope through a brake or Munter knot on one end, but a pulley system isn't necessary. The rope is supposed to hang a few feet below the line; the tape will do the rest. Tape the rope to the webbing every 3 feet or so—once or twice around is plenty—and you're ready to start training.

Waterlining

In my opinion long waterlines are hands down the best preparation for highlining. Waterlines are some of the hardest slacklines to walk, which makes them perfect for training. Slackliners typically find it impossible or extremely difficult to walk waterlines that would be well within their abilities on land. Even though we're not aware of it, the mind constantly takes visual cues from our surroundings, making thousands of minute adjustments in posture every day just to keep us balanced during normal activities. Most of these visual cues come from the ground, which is flat, fills most of our peripheral vision, and never moves. When water stretches in all directions, the mind struggles to orient the body; its main reference point is in a state of constant motion, making balance nearly impossible.

The only way to send a waterline is by focusing on the few good spatial references our mind has left. The slackline itself and the anchors, as well as possibly the horizon, are all that's left in a once crowded field of visual cues, but we still have the physical cues as on any other line. The pull of gravity on our bodies and the feeling of the slackline under our feet is exactly the same as on any other line. When I'm waterlining—as well as highlining— I find myself focusing inward, consciously shifting my awareness from where it normally resides (behind my eyes) down to my center of balance. I think of this center as behind my belly button. From there it's easy to be more aware of shifting

abdominal muscles, flexing thighs, and waving arms that tell me where my body is in space and keep me balanced.

It's impossible to completely block out the water under a waterline, or the exposure around a highline; you would have to close your eyes altogether to do it. However, it is possible to focus your attention elsewhere. My world shrinks when I'm on a highline; my eyes never move from the anchor, and I become very aware of my body, my breath, and the sensation of the line. I focus on the way it feels to balance, and on reaching the anchor locked in my sights; everything else just fades away. It's kind of like having an intimate conversation in a crowded room: You're aware of people speaking all around you, but you can only understand one speaker at a time. The crowd noise seems to fade when you focus on a single person. Waterlines build the skill of selective focus, forcing you to balance with your body and learn to block out distraction. Long waterlines are better training than short; you know your training line is the right length when it's a challenge to walk. Sometimes you learn the most on the slacklines that you *don't* send. Training isn't about sending, it's about how many hours you work to get better.

Highline Toproping

The most mentally challenging aspect of highlining is the potential for taking a leash fall, known as a whipper. Leash falls swing the highliner around and below the line. In order to avoid the potential for a whipper, many slackliners walk their first highline "on toprope." A highline toprope is simply a second line made of wire, webbing, or rope that is anchored 8 to 10 feet above the highline and tensioned. The student can clip into this line, eliminating the possibility of a leash fall.

GEAR

- A piece of static rope or cable
- Anchor materials for a set of complex anchors
- A highlining leash or daisy-chain
- A pulley or rings

To build a highline toprope, you must choose a location that offers a second set of anchors 8 to 10 feet above the highline anchors. Trees work well. Build an anchor on each side and tension the toprope exactly as you would a highline; remember to back up your anchor materials. The toprope is a lifesaving device, so rig accordingly.

Personal Gear

Most highlining gear is shared, with everyone taking turns on the line. However, there are a few personal items that you will be expected to have, and a few extras that might make your first day a little easier.

HARNESS

Don't show up at a highline without your own harness. Nobody really likes to share; it's dangerous to change harnesses near the edge; and most highliners keep theirs on between walks for convenience. It's important to bring a harness that fits your body correctly. The waistband should cinch securely at belly-button level, and the leg loops should fit snugly around the tops of your thighs. A loose-fitting or low-rise harness can spell disaster for any highliner; you want it to make you feel safe, not as if you could fall out.

Andy Lewis sending a waterline in Thailand

Florian Herla uses many pieces of specialized equipment while attempting to walk this highline.

QUICKDRAWS

The only way to fully rest on a highline is by hanging below the line sitting in a harness. The leash would put you too far beneath the webbing if you were to hang from the end, but you can clip in close to the line using a quickdraw or a carabiner linked to the belay loop of your harness and the leash rings. A resting hang is helpful between attempts, and the quickdraw will save you when you are too freaked out or your arms are tired from catching. The quickdraw will also help you slide back to the anchor more easily from the center of the line.

Emily Sukiennik resting beneath the line after a fall. The hanging ladder is used to climb back up to the line after a fall to the end of the leash. Climbing back to the line takes a surprising amount of upper body strength; clipping a ladder to the rings can make remounting much easier.

ANDY LEWIS

HELMET

It's a good idea for beginners to wear helmets. If you take a whipper too close to the end of the highline, it's technically possible to swing and hit the cliff's edge. Mounting can be done safely by scooting well away from the cliff before standing, but a fall near the cliff at the end of your send can be dangerous.

SHOES AND GLOVES

Consider protecting your hands and feet when highlining. Gloves are a no-brainer; you'll be hanging from sharp, tensioned webbing, so gloves will protect your hands and add extra grip for catching. Highliners are more divided about shoes. I was a barefoot highliner for years, and I always tangled my toes in the leash falling or cut my feet on rocks at the edge, but some slackers can't walk confidently in shoes. I like to protect my feet with slacklining shoes; I can slack longer and more confidently. Training with shoes prepares you to slackline in a wider range of environments, and makes cold-weather slacking possible.

That said, wear whatever makes you comfortable enough to relax and send. I met a man named Boswell once, who insisted on highlining in socks. His technique was to slide his front foot forward between each step; he told me he had the first "socked send" of Lost Arrow Spire. Anything goes in highlining; the trick is finding out what makes you feel best on the line.

Managing Fear

Highlining is a two-part challenge: mind and body. Regardless of how physically fit a slackliner is, he or she will not be able to send a highline unless mentally prepared to face the exposure. Though often described in terms of height, exposure is actually how high you *perceive* yourself to be. It's not just a fear of being far from the ground—though there is that. It's more like having an ocean of space around you. Humans have a primal fear of exposure so deeply rooted in the mind that it can paralyze even the best slackliner. I've watched slackers sit on the line for as much as an hour, willing themselves to stand. They just cannot make their body go through with it. This fear subsides as you spend more time on the line. I still get jitters from the space below me on a highline; it doesn't ever completely go away, but it does get easier. There are a few things you can do to help your mind adjust and relax when the exposure is overwhelming.

If you're seriously considering walking a highline, or if you've already attempted one, you should be encouraged because the battle is half won—your conscious mind has accepted the idea. The challenge now is convincing the rest of your brain to go along with it. The brain is capable of putting the body in a physical state that makes slacklining almost impossible. The survival instinct goes into overdrive, adrenaline starts pumping, and heart rate and respiration accelerate; all these symptoms make it difficult to slackline.

It can be enormously helpful in your highlining progression to simply tie in, scoot out a few feet, and sit on the line for a few minutes. You will be amazed by the difference between sitting on the cliff's edge and sitting on the line. Start by tying into the highline leash, then clip your belay loop to the leash rings with a carabiner or quickdraw. Clipping in short to the rings will allow you to more easily reach the webbing, controlling your weight with your arms. Slide out to the middle of the gap,

Michael Payton gets comfortable with the line before attempting to walk in high winds.

Sitting in my poised position to gather courage on a training highline in Fruita, Colorado

Cassie Frantz hanging from Terry Acomb's practice highline

hanging below the line. This is the most restful position really possible on a highline.

Once you're out there, take in the exposure and attempt to get comfortable. Get into your poised position and breathe deeply. Try hanging from your knees, or unclip your quickdraw from the line and hang from your hands; from there you can even try letting go into a leash fall. Sometimes getting this first fall out of the way can make things a little easier; practicing will show you that the fall is actually nothing to be afraid of.

It may take a while to get used to the feeling of exposure around you. Some lines are more exposed than others; the least exposed lines are tree highlines and short highlines. The most exposed are long, high tower highlines. Starting out on lower lines with less exposure is a good idea for beginners.

That wasn't so bad! Hanging from the line with both arms extended reduces the length of the whipper. Letting go from here sets you down onto your leash fairly gently.

Doing laps on Terry Acomb's practice highline, only about 40 feet high. It's easy to spot details on the ground at this height, and beginners will be much more comfortable on a lower-elevation highline.

Highline Mounts

Many highlines require a sitting mount: This means you must be able to maintain a poised position on the line and stand without touching anything but the line itself. Essentially a static trick, mounting is technically the most difficult part of a highline walk—or it can be if you're not prepared. Mounting is a great mental challenge because it's the moment where you finally commit to standing, trying to balance on a skinny rope stretched across a gorge. Your mind is sending a million years' worth of conditioned pleas for self-preservation to your frontal lobe; just dealing with that is enough to send most people back to the edge of the cliff. I've coached dozens of first-time highliners through those moments, watching them sit poised, willing themselves to mount and struggling to muster up

Highline pioneer Scott Turpin mounting a line in Utah

enough courage to do so. You want your mount to be second nature so you can focus all your energy on the mental game.

You are much more likely to commit to standing if it is a motion you are comfortable doing. A Chongo mount or any other sit start variation will work. The important thing is to train yourself to mount using nothing other than the slackline for assistance. Pick the mount you like best and use it every single time you get on a slackline so that it becomes effortless. You're ready to highline if you can do a successful sit start with no hesitation, every single try.

A drop-knee start

A Chongo mount

Mounting with a Leash

It's easy to get tangled in the leash during mounting. Always position the leash carefully while resting in your poised position, and push the leash rings as far as possible back toward the anchor behind you.

For side leash wearers, drape the leash over the leg where it's clipped so that it connects to the rings behind your back. For between the legs wearers, let the leash hang straight down between both legs, running in front of the line and back to the rings behind your back foot.

Frederick Zimmerman mounts the Yosemite Falls Highline with a left side leash. To keep it out of the way, he mounts with his left foot forward, draping the leash over and behind his leg.
HAYLEY ASHBURN

Catching

Catching can be pretty intimidating on a highline, but if you practice at home a few times it will be no big deal. A good catch is going to be really important on your first few highlines, where you'll probably be falling a lot. Catching the line means grabbing it as

you fall to prevent whipping or falling to the end of your leash. It is always preferable to catch because it shows that you have control, and because it takes less energy to remount the line. After a whipper you'll need to climb your leash all the way back up to the line, which will tire you out very quickly and reduce the number of attempts you can make at sending.

Florian Herla demonstrates how catching the line can conserve energy.

You may take a dozen or more falls before sending a challenging highline. If you can save energy during your falls by catching the line correctly, you will have more chances to send the highline.

Key Points for Catching

- Spot the line.
- Catch with both hands.
- Pull the line in toward your chest.
- Wrap both legs around the line.

Practicing at home before you try it on a highline will help build the muscle memory you need to catch quickly. Spotting your catch is difficult on a highline because looking for the line forces you to look down. But if you don't focus on the line beneath you, it will be impossible to grab it with both hands. Pulling the line into your chest as you fall will prevent you from swinging out and away from the line. You want your center of gravity as close as possible to the line to make it easier to hold on. Simply spreading your legs slightly as you fall will help keep the line close to your body, and it's much easier to catch with both arms and legs. Always avoid catching with one arm or leg. Deemed the "chicken-wing," this move can be very painful; think about wearing pants and long sleeves to your first highline to minimize injuries from catching.

To practice basic highline catching and mounting skills, rig a trickline at shoulder height and position some padding underneath the line. Practice slowly catching to get used to reaching straight down for the line. If you can commit this position to muscle memory, catching will be a breeze.

Ouch! This is a chicken-wing—avoid at all costs! Always catch with both hands and legs.

Practice spotting the line and catching in slow motion at home.

Getting Back on the Line

Remounting the line after a fall takes a lot of upper body strength. If you're not a climber, practice mantling on your slackline at home. You'll be surprised by how much energy it takes to mantle with no footholds.

Tying In

Tying into the highline system keeps athletes from falling to the ground. The rare highliner will walk a line free solo, or without a leash, but for most of us, tying in is an easy way to make highlining safer. Highliners tie into their lines with a short piece of dynamic material called a leash. Secured to the athlete's harness with a figure eight follow-through—just like a climber ties into a rope—the leash slides along the highline on two rings and drags behind the walker as he or she crosses the line. A leash can make highlining incredibly safe; because the leash follows along behind the slacker, he or she will never fall more than a few short feet below the line, no matter where in the walk a whip occurs.

If you fall without catching, you will take a whipper, speeding past the line and hanging by your leash a short distance below. It's always safer to catch than it is to whip because whippers put large loads on the gear, and friction between the leash rings and slackline can damage the webbing. Leashes are a fail-safe and, like everything else in a highline system, must be redundant.

There are two types of redundant leashes: double leashes, which are made from two short sections of climbing rope taped together; and threaded

Two figure eight knots are used by this highliner to protect a fall.

A leash correctly tied to two leash rings
ANDY LEWIS COLLECTION

leashes, which are made from 9.2 millimeter dynamic rope threaded through ¹¹⁄₁₆-inch tubular webbing.

You must at least know how to correctly tie in with a leash in order to begin walking highlines.

One end of the leash (or leashes) ties to both leash rings with a figure eight follow-through. Tie a figure eight onto the leash about an arm's length from the end. Pass the tail through both rings and follow through the figure eight. When tying into a double leash made from two climbing ropes, both ropes should pass through both rings.

It is not necessary to back up the figure eights if the tail is more than twice the length of the knot itself. If you have too much tail, tie a half fisherman's knot or a Yosemite backup to keep extra rope out of your way when walking.

Next, link the leash to your harness with a figure eight. The position of this knot will determine the length of your leash, so pay attention—too close

A double leash made from two pieces of dynamic rope tied to the harness with figure eight knots and Yosemite backups

to the rings and you'll get tangled in the leash, too far and you could take a big whipper. The leash should be slightly longer than the length of your leg. After tying a figure eight, pass the end of the leash through your harness. Both types of leash must pass through two "hard points" on the harness. Find the hard points on your harness by locating the belay loop, a hard ring of nylon hanging at the waist. The belay loop passes through both hard points; tie your leash correctly by following the path of the belay loop through the harness. Pass the tail of the knot through both hard points on your harness and follow through the figure eight. Back up your knot with a Yosemite follow-through or a half fisherman's knot.

Leash Management

The leash can be worn between the legs or to one side. Between the legs leashes are the safest choice for beginners; to wear a side leash you must accurately predict which way you'll fall, and this can be difficult for beginners. However, some highliners simply feel more comfortable with a side leash; walk with a leash worn both ways at home on a lowline to choose your style.

Wearing the leash positioned in between the legs will ensure a comfortable fall in any direction. To minimize the bulkiness of the leash between the legs, tie a sleek, well-dressed knot and consider using a thinner leash material. Position the figure eight as close as possible to your harness. Tie the tail with a Yosemite backup instead of a half fisherman's, and tuck the excess into the waistband of your harness.

To wear the leash to one side, tuck the rope into your leg loop where it crosses the side of your leg. You can also rig a clip or Velcro to hold the leash in place while walking. The leash must come free of the clip during a fall so that it catches the slacker in the center of the harness. Use something weak enough to release under body weight, or you will end up hanging sideways. A piece of tape, Velcro, or a loose rubber band will work.

Clip the leash so that it hangs comfortably on the *opposite* side of the one to which you normally

A leash worn between the legs

A leash worn to the side

fall. If you prefer to fall left, wear your leash on the right. This will prevent your body parts from tangling with the leash during a whipper.

THE LEASH DANCE

Many new highliners struggle with their leashes. When faced with so much intimidating new input, it's easy to get distracted perfecting the leash. This is called the leash dance, and it's a convenient way to stall before walking the highline. Most of us will look for any excuse to delay our turn on the line; we'll adjust our clothing, hair, harness, and leash two or three times each before scooting out on the line. Even after years of highlining, I find myself resisting the urge to look down and check my leash as I stand up.

In order to be comfortable with your leash, build your own and practice tying into it, then

mounting and walking on lowlines. Definitely double- and triple-check your leash knots, but do it before you scoot out on the line. Hanging in the exposure while you do your leash dance will only increase your anxiety and make it harder to send.

> ## Key Points for Highline Leashes
>
> - Must be redundant (two pieces of rope or threaded webbing).
>
> - Must tie to two leash rings, never carabiners.
>
> - Must tie through both hard points on harness.

Highline Rigging

There is a lot to learn about highline rigging—whole books have been written on climbing anchors alone. Reading this guide is a good step toward learning how to safely rig highlines, but you should rig several highlines with a more experienced slackliner before rigging a highline alone. There are dozens of ways to rig a highline system, but many are interchangeable. You only need to know one or two, especially since you can only use one method at a time. As you rig more highlines, you'll discover that it's *fun* to learn new and creative ways to use your gear. You don't need to start your journey knowing every knot, hitch, and strength rating out there. Take the time to learn a few fundamentals, and you'll have the tools to safely learn from your experience in the field.

I've included as much reliable theoretical and field-tested information as possible to support the rigging strategies recommended in this guide, but my personal experience has a far greater impact on the way I rig slacklines than anything I learned from a book. If you're feeling a little confused by all the technical discussion, remember this: Safe rigging comes down to anticipating risks and preparing for the worst possible scenario.

Highline Anchor Building

The first highline I ever attempted was the Lost Arrow Spire Highline in Yosemite. I was a total beginner, mystified by the process of rigging, but I had been walking slacklines all summer and dreaming about the Spire. I remember sitting at the anchor on the flake side in the wind, 3,000 feet above the valley floor, looking at the four blue Camalots shoved into the crack and thinking, Is that it? I knew I should be able to make it to the other side of the line, but fear and uncertainty stopped me in my tracks. I didn't send that day, and part of the reason was that I didn't feel confident in my anchor.

Since that day the Lost Arrow Spire Highline has been forever associated with slackline anchors for me. As the first Yosemite highline, the Spire is an integral part of slacklining and highline history. I try to rig and walk the Lost Arrow Spire line every summer. I'm more confident in my anchors now,

Braden Mayfield and Andy Lewis assessing anchor potential on a stalactite in Thailand

Jenna McLennan sending the
Lost Arrow Spire Highline
ANDY LEWIS COLLECTION

because I use what I think of as the SPIRE system. All slackline anchors must be:

- **S**olid: Anchored on objects that can withstand the max force of the line.
- **P**rotected: All edges are padded to prevent abrasion.
- **I**ndependent: Anchor components are isolated from one another.
- **R**edundant: Some or all parts of the system are doubled to safeguard against failure.
- **E**qualized: Force is distributed equally on each anchor point.

Scott Turpin building a highline anchor, right

Below, the Lost Arrow Spire Highline anchor, made of four blue Camalots

HAYLEY ASHBURN

Solid

Highline anchors link several primary anchor points together to share the force of the line. Primary anchor points are things like rocks, trees, and bolts. The most important part of highline rigging is choosing primary anchor points that are *solid*.

Without solid anchor points you have nothing, regardless of how well you equalize the anchor.

The greatest force ever generated on a highline in my data set was 6,000 lbf. That's more than the weight of some pickup trucks! Remember that image when you're evaluating highline anchors.

Rigging tree highlines is a good first step for beginning highline riggers.
HAYLEY ASHBURN

TREES

Trees, when you can find them, are generally the most solid of all slackline anchors. Rig to the same size trees you would rig a longline to, paying special attention to the roots. Trees at the cliffside are suitable for highlines only if they're rooted in a good amount of soil. Trees that appear to be growing out of rocks or that look unhealthy are not solid.

BOULDERS

The density of boulders makes them great for rigging natural highline anchors. If you can sling a big boulder, this is often the most solid anchoring option. Look for blocks that are attached to the cliff and large enough to inspire confidence. If the block is not connected, it should be at least as big as a golf cart and located an adequate distance from the edge. If you're considering a detached boulder, consider the possibility of the boulder tipping; could it fall over an edge?

Most rocks can be slung with spansets safely, but watch for sharp edges. Rocks often have corners that must be padded to protect the anchor materials. Rig the spanset as low around the rock as possible, and don't rig on sloping boulders that look as if a sling would slip off the top.

This horn is solid because it's connected to the rock below and is made of granite, one of the hardest rocks in the world. It's a good shape for highline anchors because the spanset won't slip off the top.

ANDY LEWIS COLLECTION

This anchor is wrapped around a pinch between two boulders. Pinches are solid because the anchor can't slip out.

BOLTS

Climbing crags are peppered with bad bolts for highlining. You need at least three good bolts to rig a safe highline anchor. Avoid bolts smaller than half an inch. If the hangers or any part of the bolt is extremely rusty, or if the bolt spins in the hole, don't rig to it. Look at the rock quality around the bolts; if you see cratering around the bolts, don't rig to them. Highline bolts should be in good rock that's attached to the cliff. Beware of bolts installed in boulders, flakes, or bad rock. The bolt is only as solid as the rock it's drilled into.

Half-inch bolts with short sections of chain are the most common style of bolts for highlines.

This 3/8-inch rock climbing bolt is set solidly in granite; if the bolt were in soft rock like sandstone, it would not be solid enough for a highline.

CAMS, NUTS, AND OTHER CLIMBING ANCHORS

Occasionally, the only available anchor is a crack in the rocks that must be filled with spring-loaded camming devices (cams). The proper technique for placing cams falls outside the scope of this guide. Rigging highlines to camming units alone is unsafe rigging practice. The Lost Arrow Spire is the only popular highline that utilizes cams. The anchor on the cliff side is rigged to four number 3 Camalots. Because cams are not very solid, the anchor is backed up to a bolt and a tree. Never trust your life to a highline anchor made of just cams. If you must use cams, equalize as many as possible and back up to something solid like a boulder, bolts, or a tree.

Climbing cams are not designed for the constant load found in slacklining and highlining. Use extreme caution and have solid backups if using cams for your primary anchor.

Protected

Webbing is extremely strong in straight pull tests, but its flat shape makes it vulnerable to other forces. Abrasion can eat completely through the soft components of your highline in a matter of hours. The wind can make lines oscillate back and forth hundreds of times a minute, rubbing the webbing against the stone beneath like sandpaper. The movement of slackers on the line can stretch the webbing down over the sharp edge of the cliff.

Abrasion is the most dangerous force we deal with as highliners. It can affect all the soft components in our anchors, the most vulnerable being the end of the slackline between the master point and the cliff's edge.

There are two field-proven methods to combat abrasion: wrapping all soft goods to the edge of the cliff, and changing the shape of the highline with an A-frame.

PADDING

Next time you're at a highline, observe the anchors carefully while your teammates walk. Try to watch the end of the line during a big whipper too. This will give you an idea of how much each part of the anchor moves, and each element's potential for abrading against rock.

Highline gear has more potential for movement the farther away from the primary anchor point it is. Your webbing is the most vulnerable element in the system, compounded by the fact that it is the least abrasion-resistant material. Wrap the webbing in protection from the line locker to a few feet past the edge of the cliff.

A-FRAMING

Solve the root of the problem by building an A-frame between the anchor and the edge of the cliff. A highline A-frame lifts the anchor components into the air and moves vulnerable webbing farther away from the rock at cliff edges. The slackline must still somehow be protected, but the

This highline is wrapped in treewear over and past the cliff's edge. Use electrical tape to keep protection from slipping. Canyon Cain also uses treewear around his knee to protect himself while catching the line.

anchor slings are fully protected from abrasion. An A-frame prevents any movement of anchor slings by effectively separating the anchor array from the slackline.

Highline A-frames only need to be about a foot tall. They should be positioned as close to the edge of the cliff as possible, and be sturdy enough to withstand lateral forces from surfing, catching, or whipping. A moving highline can easily knock over a pile of rocks. Make your A-frame tall enough that the tensioned highline will put adequate downward force on the structure. The pressure of the line squeezing the A-frame down against the ground will keep it secure. Put your A-frame in place before tensioning, then pad the structure. If you tension and there's not enough pressure on the A-frame, or if your structure looks unstable, have a friend lift the line while you pile more rocks or padding on the frame to make it taller. You may not even realize you need an A-frame until your line is tensioned, or your A-frame may collapse under tension. If this happens, have someone lift the line while you slide a structure underneath.

Independent and Redundant

To safely rig highlines, you must be able to anticipate risk, thinking ahead to exactly what would happen if any individual piece of the system failed. Redundancy is simple; the credo is "Never trust your life to a single piece of gear." Every part of the highline system, including the webbing across the gap and the complex anchors on each side are redundant. Redundancy guarantees that there are doubles of every piece in the system. The doubles are called

backups. Each part of the system has a main and a backup. There are a main and a backup anchor on each side, a main and a backup slackline, even main and backup line lockers. The highline system is considered independent when the failure of any main component would not compromise the backup.

Highline anchors will usually require a compromise between the values of equalized, independent, and redundant.

Equalized

All the slackline anchors we've built so far have been simple anchors, those that wrap a single point like a tree. Highlines are built with complex anchor systems. Complex anchors link several primary anchor points together with a static rope or spanset. This shares the load between points and safeguards the highline from failure in case any single anchor point fails.

The number of points equalized depends on how solid each point seems. Equalizing can't compensate for bad primary anchor points, but can

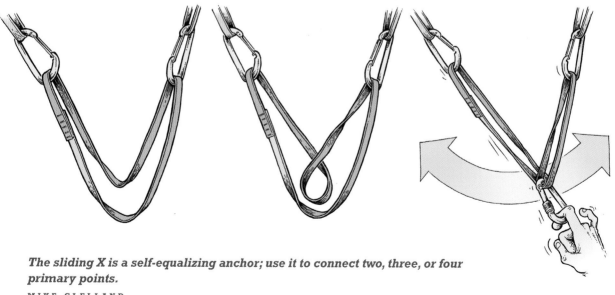

The sliding X is a self-equalizing anchor; use it to connect two, three, or four primary points.

MIKE CLELLAND

How to Build a Sliding X to Three Points

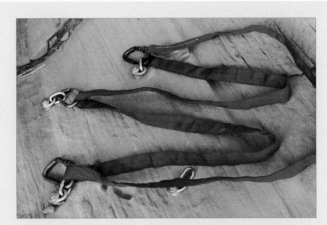

Step 1

Step 2

Step 3

make any anchor stronger by distributing the load of the slackline.

When your primary anchor points are less than ideal, equalization is essential. You can think of an equalized anchor like a group of slackliners hauling on a pulley rope to get a slackline tight. The more slackliners pull on the rope, the less work each individual has to do. However, just like pulling tension with a group of slackliners, it's very difficult to tell exactly what percentage of the total work each primary anchor point is doing. To test the equalization of your anchor after tensioning, feel the relative stiffness of each arm. Stiffer arms are holding more.

THE V-ANGLE

The V-angle is the angle between each set of arms in the anchor sling. Perfect equalization occurs only if the V-angle is 20 degrees or less. Any angle greater than 40 degrees multiplies the load on the master point rather than distributing it between several points. Set the master point as far away from the anchors as possible so that the V-angles in the sling achieve better equalization.

JUDGING THE DIRECTION OF PULL

It's important to pay close attention to where you place the master point of your anchor. After tensioning, the slackline will pull the master point straight in the direction of the opposite anchor.

If you tie your master point too far left or right, the slackline will move it, destroying the equalization of your anchor. To build a safe, equalized anchor, you must predict the direction of pull by using the anchor on the opposite side as a guide. The arms of your anchor should point to the opposite anchor.

Pay attention to the angles in your anchor sling and keep them between 20 and 40 degrees.
MIKE CLELLAND

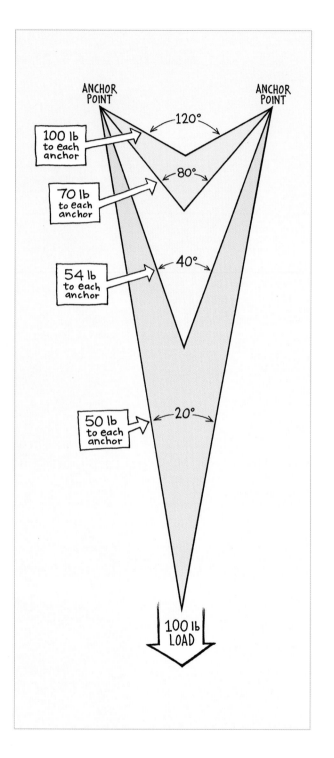

To accurately adjust the direction of pull, hold one arm of the anchor in each hand and lean backwards, spotting the opposite anchor.

A Static Rope Anchor

Make a sliding X–style anchor with a static rope by threading the end of the rope through all four chain links and pulling down each as you did with the other sliding X anchors. To make any sliding X anchor independent, tie an overhand or figure eight knot with all the loops just above the master point. An independent anchor does not spread the load evenly between each arm, so this anchor sacrifices equalization for independence, but the bolts are solid so the anchor is solid. Tying the knot also makes the master point a redundant loop, which means I can safely clip both the main line and the backup to this anchor.

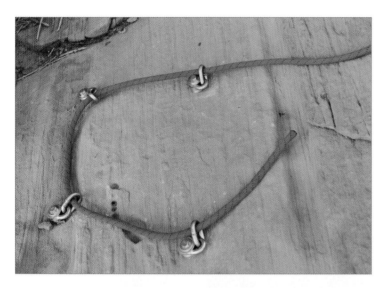

Threading a static rope through highline bolts

Tying a double fisherman's knot to secure a static rope anchor sling

Pulling down on the loops to equalize between four bolts

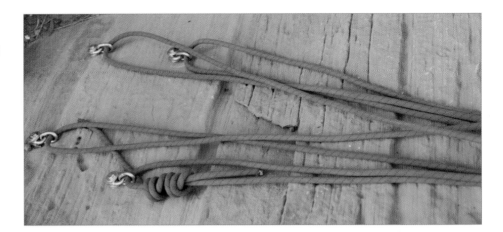

An enormous figure eight at the master point makes each arm of the anchor sling independent and creates a redundant anchor loop with several independent strands of rope.

Clip both the main and backup lines to this master point to rig a highline.

Spanset Anchors

It is difficult to equalize many anchor points with a spanset because of the bulkiness of the material. Instead, make two independent anchors, one each for the main slackline and the backup.

Once the lines are properly connected to both the main and backup master points, you can tie off the extra webbing and/or rope to an unused bolt for added security.

The purple anchor will hold the main line, the green the backup, each on separate master points. The master points must be positioned close together so that the highline will move as little as possible in the event of one anchor failing.

Clip both the backup rope and the tail of the slackline to the backup bolt.

Each step in highlining needs to be taken seriously.

Highlining Efficiently: A Step-by-Step Guide

The key to highlining efficiently is to plan ahead and prepare. By planning well and preparing for the highline ahead of time, you can use more of your time at the crag for rigging. There are a few things you can do the night before a highline mission that will make things go much more quickly and smoothly. Briefly sketch your highline and make a gear list. The average highline requires around thirty-five individual pieces of gear—that's a lot to remember. Forgetting essential gear is one of the most common mistakes for highliners of all ability levels. Drawing things out will help, especially if you are still unfamiliar with the highline system.

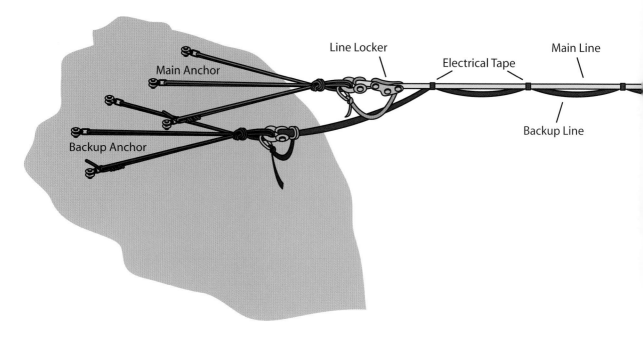

Anatomy of a highline (labels: Main Anchor, Backup Anchor, Line Locker, Electrical Tape, Main Line, Backup Line)

Gear

- Webbing
- Backup rope or backup webbing
- Electrical tape
- Spansets or rope for four anchors
- Steel locking carabiners
- Four line lockers (rings and steel locking biners or shackles)
- Pulleys
- Line protection and edge padding
- Two steel leash rings 2.5 inches or larger in diameter
- Highline leash
- Harness

Pre-rigging

The main and backup slacklines will be taped together so that they have the look and feel of a single line. Many riggers tape the lines together once they've both been anchored, by sliding across the lines and hanging in their harness over the highline gap. You can save a big headache by taping your lines together at home and then coiling the highline together in your bag. Use plain electrical tape for highlines; it generally sticks only to itself, allowing you to adjust the tension of the line as you go without ruining the tape. Duct tape or climbing tape has too much adhesion and can leave sticky residue on your line. It helps to use a contrasting color for a visual aid while you're sending. Tape should be spaced about 3 feet apart. This is also a very smart time to thread the leash and leash rings onto the line so that you don't forget them later.

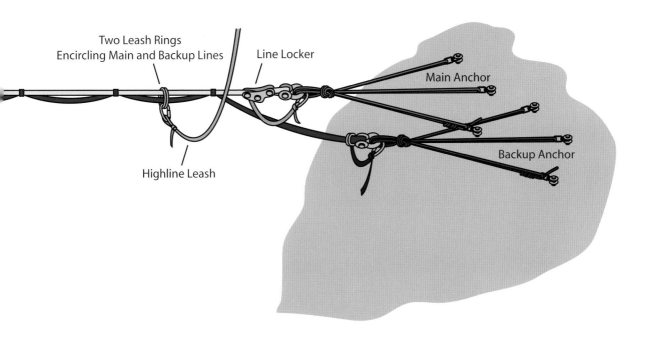

Two Leash Rings
Encircling Main and Backup Lines   Line Locker

Main Anchor

Backup Anchor

Highline Leash

Getting the Line Across

Build the main anchor on each side before trying
to get the line across. The highline can be heavy
and difficult to hold if your hands are full with
anchor-building gear. Getting the line across will be
different for every highline; sometimes you'll need
to climb, sometimes you'll be able to walk around,
sometimes you might have to throw a weight
across. Regardless of the conditions I recommend
to always use a long piece of thick string initially,
because you might be dragging the string along the
ground or over bushes and rocks. Once the string is
across the gap, the person on the side with the webbing can tie the end of the pre-taped highline to
the string and you can start pulling the line across.
Now you can work together on getting the slackline flat and into the line lockers on both sides.

Tensioning Highlines

Before you tension, make sure that the rings and
leash are on the highline and that the anchors are
clear of extra gear that may get stuck as anchors
stiffen. Insert protection and A-frames if necessary.
The backup anchor should be fully rigged on the
static side and clipped in loosely on the tensioning side. Tension with your pulleys as you normally
would. It is safe to leave your pulleys in the highline
system during walking, but you must back up the
pulleys by tying a knot in the tail of the main line
and clipping it to the master point. The backup
rope can be tensioned by hand. If you over-tension
the backup rope, it will feel uncomfortable for
walking. You'll get a feel for the backup rope tension—highliners have different preferences.

Backing Up

Clip the backup rope to the backup anchor with a figure eight on a bight, and double-check all the locking carabiners before walking. Reevaluate the webbing at the edges to determine if they need more protection before walking.

A highline with a backup rope taped beneath
HAYLEY ASHBURN

Getting the line across at Taft Point in Yosemite, California
HAYLEY ASHBURN

Tensioning with pulleys can get difficult on highlines, but soft-pointing can make it easier.
HAYLEY ASHBURN

A highline being tensioned with a linegrip. The linegrip should never be left in a highline system. This line will be soft-pointed, removing both pulleys and linegrip before walking.

A view of the highline before releasing tension to remove the pulleys. You must finalize the master point before soft-pointing a highline anchor.

The backup rope and webbing should be tied to a second master point that is independent from the main line, in this case a separate biner on a redundant master point.

HAYLEY ASHBURN

De-tensioning

De-tensioning should be very easy and fast compared to tensioning. The only crucial thing to remember is *to untie all your backup knots and anchors before releasing tension.* If you release the tension of the slackline with the backups still tied, you'll have to re-tension the slackline to get the backups out, and that's an enormous pain. Use the string to pass the slackline back to a partner on the other side and you're finished!

The backup rope and webbing are tied again to an extra bolt we found some ways from the main anchor. This isn't necessary, but it's better to have it and not need it, than need it and not have it.

HAYLEY ASHBURN

Glossary

anchor: the solid object the slackline is connected to, such as a tree; also commonly used to refer to anchor slings

anchor slings: rope or webbing that wraps around your anchor

BASE jump: an acronym that stands for the various objects a jumper can make a parachute exit from: B–building, A–antenna, S–span (bridge), E–earth (cliff)

BASEline: in which you make a BASE exit (parachute jump) off a highline

beta: a climbing term meaning information; gaining prior information about a climb or line

butt-bounce: a dynamic trick in slacklining; bouncing off the line from one's butt and landing back on the line

carabiner: a link used in climbing and slacklining to securely attach webbing to slings or bolts; made of steel or aluminum in non-locking and locking varieties

dynamic: characterized by movement, change, or stretch

dynamic end: the end of the line that holds a tensioning system between the anchor and the line locker (the location of the line locker on this side will change)

first-across (FA): a slacklining achievement accomplished by walking a line that has never been walked before. FA is also used in climbing to mean "first ascent," or the first time a rock climbing route has been completed by an individual.

flashline: a slackline rigged, walked, and taken down very quickly, usually to avoid the notice of public authorities when slacking on public property

free solo (FS): to walk a highline without safety equipment such as a leash and harness

full-man send (or full-babe): a slacklining accomplishment in which the athlete walks the line from anchor to anchor once in each direction

highline: a slackline that is higher than it is long, or sufficiently high to require the use of a leash and harness

highwire: commonly referred to as a "tightrope"; made of steel cable and anchored not only at each end, but at intervals along the wire, using supporting wires called cavallettis

jibbing: a slackline trick where the athlete hops several times in a row without stopping

kilonewton (kN): unit used to rate most slackline gear. One kN is equal to 1,000 newtons. Because newtons are based on motion and pound-force is based on earth's gravity, it is impossible to precisely convert one to the other. However, as long as you're rigging here on earth, it's safe to say that 1kN is approximately equal to 225 pounds.

leash: a line, 4 feet or more in length, used to link a highliner's harness to a titanium ring that slides along as the athlete walks a highline. A leash prevents highliners from falling to their death in the event of a "whipper," or big fall.

line locker: a ring, chain link, or device that holds the end of the slackline flat using friction

Highliners having fun on a "spaceline" during a partial solar eclipse

mechanical advantage: the ratio of force applied to a machine to the force produced by it. Pulleys and ratchets give riggers a mechanical advantage by multiplying the force of humans cranking a ratchet or pulling rope to pull tension on a line.

minimum breaking strength (MBS): the lowest force required to break the gear

monkey: a term of respect referring to fearless slackliners or climbers. The first monkeys were the original climbers in Yosemite in the 1960s and 1970s. Today the term is used to describe slackliners both because of their Yosemite history and the Gibbon mascot (which is technically an ape, but close enough).

multiplier: a pulley and a tibloc or prusik that links to pulleys, multiplying mechanical advantage

newton: the international standard for measuring force. One newton is the amount of force required to accelerate a one kilogram object at a rate of 1 meter per second squared. A newton is about 0.25 pound, the weight of a steel carabiner.

on-sight (OS): a slackline achievement accomplished by sending a line on the first try, or "on first sight"

prana: Sanskrit for the life force or breath energy; a force tapped into by successful slackliners and all athletes to focus and achieve goals

primary anchor points: environmental anchors for slackline rigging, usually trees

racking gear: the process of organizing and setting aside the various pieces of gear needed to rig a slackline

rappel ring or rap ring: a 1-inch steel or aluminum ring used in climbing to aid rappelling; standard gear in slacklining used for line lockers

ratchet: a device consisting of a bar with metal teeth that turns in one direction only; a tensioning device used in slacklining to gain mechanical advantage

rigging: building a slackline or other structure

rope walking: balancing on ropes; differs from slacklining in that the medium is round and rolls beneath the foot

send: to walk a slackline from anchor to anchor without falling

slackline: a piece of flat webbing stretched between two points and tensioned

slackwire: an un-tensioned, un-guyed wire for walking

soft point: to remove the tensioning system from a slackline after it is properly tensioned

static: characterized by a lack of movement, change, or stretch

static end: the end of the line without a tensioning system

swami-belt: a type of highline leash, knotted and tied around the walker's waist, that eliminates the need for a harness. Used by advanced highliners only, the swami-belt increases the consequences of a whipper, creating a more painful fall than that experienced using a harness.

tightrope: a tensioned rope used for rope walking; commonly misused to refer to highwires

whipper: a fall taken on a highline, where the athlete does not catch the line, but falls, swinging to the end of his or her leash

wire walking: the art of walking on wires of any sort

Knots Index

Knot Terminology

Bight: A fold or loop in the rope/webbing

Standing end: Part of the rope/webbing not used to tie the knot

Tail: The unused, non-load-bearing section of rope/webbing that hangs outside the knot

Working end: The section of rope being twisted into a knot

Guide to Knots

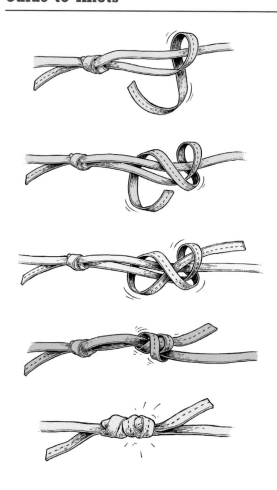

A double fisherman's knot is useful for connecting two ends of rope or webbing, or for making a continuous loop out of rope for a slackline anchor.

MIKE CLELLAND

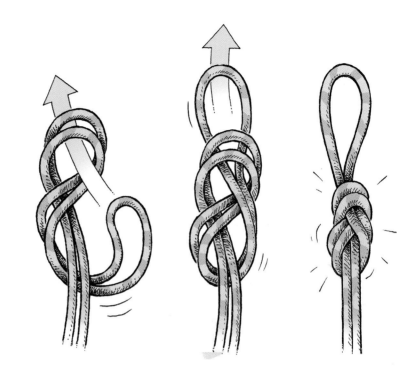

The figure eight on a bight can be used to make loops in static rope for a slackline anchor or backup rope.
MIKE CLELLAND

The girth hitch with a bight release, tied only in webbing, is used for making line lockers and webbing anchors.

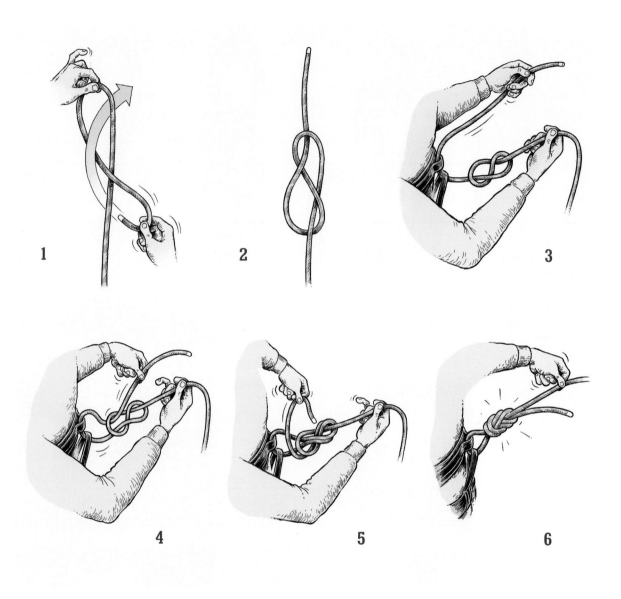

1

2

3

4

5

6

The threaded figure eight with a Yosemite backup is the standard knot for tying into highlines.
MIKE CLELLAND

Thread a Yosemite backup knot this way after tying in with a figure eight.

The half fisherman's knot is used as a backup to a figure eight.

The Bowline is a great knot to use when backing up your webbing or rope.

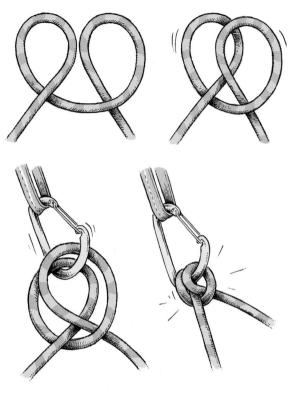

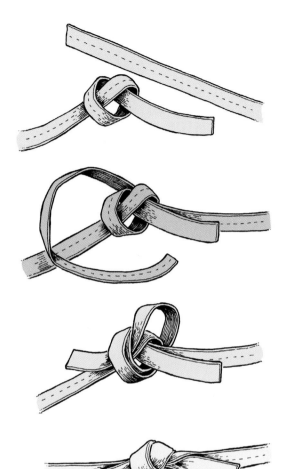

Tying a clove hitch.

MIKE CLELLAND

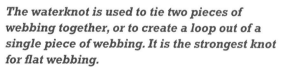

The waterknot is used to tie two pieces of webbing together, or to create a loop out of a single piece of webbing. It is the strongest knot for flat webbing.

MIKE CLELLAND

The overhand on a bight is used to tie webbing into a looped end for backup.

MIKE CLELLAND

Index

Page numbers in bold indicate photos and illustrations

About the Author

Hayley Ashburn is a NOLS-trained outdoor educator who has used her experience as a rock climbing guide to teach slacklining and highline rigging since 2009. Winner of the 2010 trickline women's World Cup, Hayley worked for several years as an athlete for Gibbon Slacklines, tricklining and highlining at events across Europe and the United States. Her first book, *Modern Slacklining,* was published in 2011. In *How to Slackline!,* Hayley uses her experience to expand on her first book, moving past basic slacklining to cover topics in advanced rigging and slackline training. Hayley has spent the last several years in Moab, Utah, establishing new highlines and working with her team, the Moab Monkeys, to rig adventure highlines such as the Leviathan, the world's highest and longest tower highline, and A Test of Fate, on the nation's tallest freestanding tower, The Titan, at Utah's Desert Towers.

About the Photographer

Scott Rogers is a professional slackliner specializing in adventure photography and videography. With ten years of slacklining experience, he brings his creative vision to this one-of-a-kind book. *How to Slackline!* includes images of slacklines from around the world. His personal accomplishments include the highest elevation highline in North America, the longest highline in Brazil, and the first underground highline. He is one of very few people in the world to have BASE jumped off a highline. His images have been featured in *Nat. Geo. Adventure, Rock & Ice, New York Times, L.A. Times,* and numerous other print and digital publications around the world. He currently lives in Moab, Utah, due to the close proximity and high concentration of world-class highlines and BASE jumps.

Your next adventure begins here.

falcon.com

PROTECTING CLIMBING ACCESS SINCE 1991

ACCESS FUND

| JOIN US |
WWW.ACCESSFUND.ORG

Jonathan Siegrist, Third Millenium (14a), the Monastery, CO. Photo by: Keith Ladzinski